THE 7 DAY PRACTICE ROUTINE FOR GUITARISTS

*CHORDS
*SCALES
*ARPEGGIOS
*MUSIC THEORY
*EXERCISES
*FOR ALL GUITARISTS

80+ PAGES

Lifein12Keys.com

Introduction 5

The Right Tools 6

How To Use This Book................................7

Electric or Acoustic? 8

Printing & Sharing 9

Beginners, Intermediate and Advanced 10

Monday - PRacticing, Warmups & Picking 11

Thoughts on Practicing...............................12

4 Note-per-string exercise...........................13

Chordal Picking 14

Villa-Lobos Picking Study 16

Double-Triplets with Speed Bursts 19

Monday Routine Roundup 21

Tuesday - The Modal Workout 22

What is a Mode?..22

3 Note-Per-String Modes 24

Modal Shapes..24

The Modal Workout 26

Diatonic Arpeggios Inside Modes 29

The Modal Workout 30

Tuesday Routine Roundup 33

Wednesday - Arpeggios..34

Triads...34

5 String Diatonic Arpeggios 36

Arpeggio Workout......................................37

    Diatonic 7th Arpeggios 39

    7th Arpeggio Shapes: 40

    Wednesday Routine Roundup 43

Thursday - Scales 44

    What is a Scale? 44

    The Circle of Keys: 45

    The Sharp Side 47

    The Flat Side 48

    FAQ: Guitarists on Scales 49

    Scale Theory 51

    Minor Scale 51

    Harmonic Minor 53

    Melodic Minor 53

    Modern (Jazz) Melodic Minor 54

    3 Note Per String Minor Shapes: 56

    Scale Sequence example 58

    Thursday Routine roundup 60

Friday - Chords 61

    7th Chords 63

    Diatonic 7th Chord Study 63

    The Diminished "Connector" 66

    Chord Formula Master Chart 68

Saturday - Classical Guitar 101 70

    Classical Guitar Slurs: Hammer & Pulls 71

    Slurs 71

    The Spider Sequence 75

Sunday - 120 Arpeggio Studies 77

    Classical Guitar Scales 80

Classical Scale Studies 82

Bach's Bouree in E minor 84

Beginner Chord Forms 85

Barre Chord forms 86

Pentatonic Major, Minor & Blues Shapes 88

Afterword 89

Guitar Pro Files: 89

About The Author 90

INTRODUCTION

Remember that scene in The Karate kid when after washing all of the cars and painting the fence and all of the other household chores Miyagi made Daniel do.. he turned to him and said,, ok now, show me…. PAINT THE FENCE.

At first Daniel was angry because he was asked to do all of these seemingly pointless chores that had absolutely nothing to do with Karate. Once Miyagi explained his training, the light bulb came on and Daniel finally understood his teaching methods.

I'd love to tell you it's just that easy, *but it's not*. Real Guitar technique takes time and patience and putting the work in nearly every day.

I say *nearly* every day, because you also should give your hands a rest occasionally. *Once or twice a week is sufficient to prevent injury.*

I also believe you shouldn't take more than 1 day off between good practice sessions. *The old saying is true, it's always better to play a little each day rather than cram in 6 hours on a Saturday. That's just not how good technique is developed and you will progress slowly.*

The difference between the Karate Kid metaphor and what I'm doing here is that the exercises and routines outlined in this book are actually done on the guitar, using useful musical sequences and ideas.

No wax on, wax off. Real practice, real material and really applicable theory to apply to whatever your goals are on the instrument.

That's really all I'm asking you to do here. Some repetitive chores that will yield incredible results when they are memorized and then applied to your playing.

While most guitarists may view this as a technique routine on the surface, there is quite a bit of basic harmony and music theory concepts within.

If the only things you ever learned on the guitar were the chords, scales and arpeggios in this guide, you would have enough material to write a song, improvise a solo or create a multi-part composition in any style of music at a professional level.

THE RIGHT TOOLS

Chords, scales and arpeggios are just tools in your toolbox. Sure, they're the fundamental building blocks of all things musical, but as guitarists we can utilize them in so many ways.

You need chords to play rhythm and to create songs. Scales for solos and melody and knowing *what* to play over those chords when improvising.

Arpeggios are broken chords, but playing an arpeggio in place of a scale in an improvisation gives your solos a targeted, focused sound that you won't get from scales alone. Arpeggios also help you find "blind spots" in the key that tie chords and scales together.

Practicing Chords, scales and arpeggios will boost your technique to a level where physically, everything is just easier to play. *I do mean everything*. Parts you've struggled with become easier, everything just feels better under your fingers.

You are owning the instrument.

It doesn't matter if you're a beginner or a seasoned, professional working musician. Everyone can benefit from this routine. I've done my best to include ways to tweak each daily routine to make them both easier or more difficult depending on your existing skill level.

As a working professional guitarist going on 27 years, I've changed these routines many times to not only make them better for my own playing, but also to keep them short enough to do each day. After all, we all need time to PLAY guitar after the practice. If you PRACTICE these routines weekly I guarantee your PLAYING will improve quickly and dramatically.

HOW TO USE THIS BOOK

Learn the shapes before trying the full exercises.

If you're not familiar with all 7 diatonic modes, chords or group of arpeggios, thats ok. It will come with time. On days where material is completely new to you, take that practice day to work on each shape or exercise.

Work on the shapes pertaining only to that day's practice lesson and gradually you will have committed them all to memory. After everything is memorized, you'll get the most from each day's practice session.

Always Use a Metronome.

There are a few reasons you should always practice with a metronome. The obvious being that it will set a good foundation for your timing, both in your rhythm and lead playing, as well as synchronization of both hands.

Practicing with a metronome also gives you a measurable indication of your progress in each lesson. For example if Monday's routine is too hard at 100 bpm, try knocking it down to 90 and work your way back up.

A good rule is to increase 1 bpm per day until you've reached your comfort zone at a faster tempo. Once a high threshold is reached, start about 10 below that and use that as your starting point for each day's routine.

If you're new to playing with a metronome start with 2 or 4 beats per click. When this becomes comfortable you can work on triplets and 6's as well.

If you don't have a metronome, they're pretty inexpensive. You can even download metronome apps on your computer, tablet or smart phones.

-Practice First, Play Second.

I can't stress this enough.

We all want to PLAY guitar. Save some time for playing after you PRACTICE. Always. If you only have 1 hour total time to devote to the guitar, try to split it 70/30. Practice 70% of that time then play whatever you want for the other 30%.

Use the rest day, or even a completely different session if you only want to play.

I've gotten in the habit of splitting my guitar sessions into separate afternoon and evening sessions. Typically I do that on my days off. I'll go through the daily practice routine around 1 P.M., then after dinner just play whatever I want for as long as I want with no pressure, knowing I got a good PRACTICE session in earlier.

On days when I have a gig, rehearsal or jam I'll just do the practice routine so I'm setup to do my best possible playing later. This is the habit you want to develop regardless of how much time you have to practice.

ELECTRIC OR ACOUSTIC?

This one is entirely up to you. From experience I can tell you that you can use either type of guitar for any of the routines. The possible exception being the optional fingerstyle/classical exercises on days 6 and 7 respectively. For those you should try them on a nylon string Classical style guitar if you have access to one.

If your preferred practice method is using an electric guitar and an amp I would strongly recommend alternating days between clean and dirty channels.

For example, if you're a Rock or Metal guitar player, do Tuesday's mode routine with distortion and Wednesday's arpeggios on a dry clean setting with no effects. Also 7th chords aren't going to sound great with distortion, so if you're working on those, a clean tone would work better so you can hear the voicings.

PRINTING & SHARING

I've purposely left this book in mostly "Black and White" so it can be printed and put right onto your music stand. I don't want to waste anyone's expensive ink, so I've also whenever possible, included longer music examples on their own page. This way you can simply print the pages you want without all of the text cluttering it up.

I've put a lot of time into the book, so I'd appreciate it if you did NOT share it on the internet. As an incentive, I've created an Affiliate Program for my readers and students who would like to share the book and also make some money doing it.
After your purchase, head over to http://lifein12keys.com/affiliate

I will pay you 50% of every sale. YES, 50%! All you need to do is grab your affiliate link and share on your website, social media accounts, email or wherever you like. It's all tracked automatically through SendOwl and payed right into your PayPal account.

BEGINNERS, INTERMEDIATE AND ADVANCED

Lastly, I've designed this book to be useful to Guitarists of any skill level. At a glance it may seem intimidating for a beginner.

I would advise beginning Guitarists to first absorb some of the shapes for the Chords, Scales and Arpeggios before attempting the actual music or Practice Routines.

If you're a complete beginner, try the open position chord shapes on page (86), or the Pentatonic shapes on page (87). I'd also recommend trying the 4-note-per string shape in Monday's routine right away. In over 25 years of teaching Guitar Lessons, I've had great success with students who tried this exercise on Day #1. Just do it!

For intermediate and Advanced Guitarists I think you'll find a wealth of information organized in a way that will help you get better faster.

Even for Pros, this Routine works! I've tested this stuff out on some amazing Pro Guitarist friends of mine and they all agree that an organized practice routine covering many styles, techniques and genres is beneficial to even the most seasoned Professional Guitarist.

For everyone, it may take some time to get through all of the Music Theory within this book. Take it slow and come back to things you don't quite understand. Understanding Music and Music Theory takes a lot of time. With some patience and practice, I think you'll do just fine.

Enjoy!
Craig Smith - www.Lifein12Keys.com

MONDAY - PRACTICING, WARMUPS & PICKING

One of the things I get asked the most by Guitar Students and other Guitarists both amateur and Professional is:

"What are you doing at home? What are YOU practicing?"

It's hard to give someone a straight answer without addressing a few variables. It can vary depending on a number things including what gigs I'm doing that week.

Material I may be required to work up for a future job such as a wedding or solo gig can steer my practice in a completely different direction than say a Rock or Electric gig.

If I have a lot of free time between gigs, what I practice may be vastly different than a week when I'm doing 5 or 6 gigs in a row.

One thing that never changes is my simple day-to-day technique routine. I've tweaked these daily workouts many times over the years and I think I finally have it dialed in for optimal results in the least amount of time possible.

I also may change them week to week by adding or subtracting an exercise based on my schedule. It's entirely up to you how you decide to use them.

The important thing is that you're doing something and doing it regularly. The old adage is true, it's better to practice a little each day rather than cram in 4 hours on a Saturday.

THOUGHTS ON PRACTICING

I'll typically go through the daily practice routine around 1 P.M., then after dinner just play whatever I want for as long as I want. *(Typically Classical repertoire for example.)*

With this mindset there's no pressure because I know I had a good PRACTICE session earlier.

On days when I have a gig, rehearsal or jam I'll just do the practice routine so I'm setup to do my best possible playing later.

This is the habit you want to develop regardless of how much time you have to practice.

If your preferred practice method is using an electric guitar and an amp, I would strongly recommend alternating days *(or even exercises)* between clean and dirty channels.

For example, if you're a Rock or Metal guitar player, do Tuesday's mode routine with distortion and Wednesday's Arpeggios on a dry clean setting with no effects. Next week reverse that.

I'd also recommend to those who want to use distortion to back the Gain down to a slightly uncomfortable level. Meaning, it should feel harder to play well. When you turn it back up later you'll feel that much better.

4 NOTE-PER-STRING EXERCISE

These are simple exercises you can do in front of the TV or wherever you want. No scale knowledge required here.

The basic idea is to cover all of the possible left hand finger combinations across 6 strings. At first you may want to do them in one position. After they feel comfortable, do each sequence up to the 12th position.

In the example below I've included the 1,2,3,4 sequence ascending & descending using alternate picking *(down, up)* along with the shift to the 2nd position:

When "descending" we're not going to change the order of the notes. It's still going to be fingered as 1-2-3-4! *(We'll get to 4,3,2,1 later)*

- When shifting, keep the same same finger combo (1,2,3,4) and continue up the neck.
- When you get to the 12th position start over with the next sequence (Fingers: 1,2,4,3.. **no that wasn't a typo: 1-2-4-3**).

All possible Left Hand Finger Combos in a 4 fret position:
It can take a long time to go through all the sets so alternatively you could do the "1's" this week, the "2's" next week and so on.

1234	2134	3124	4123
1243	2143	3142	4132
1324	2314	3214	4213
1342	2341	3241	4231
1423	2413	3412	4312
1432	2431	3421	4321

Time Spent: *About 30 minutes if you do one column to the 12th position. Don't forget to use a metronome!*

CHORDAL PICKING

After doing 4 note-per-string sequences I like to change it up to 1 note-per-string picking through chords. I believe there is much more benefit to changing it up this way rather than just running random scales for an hour.

There are a million variations you can play with, but the basic premise is this:
*Take any chord (**E Major** for example below) and alternate pick through it like this:*

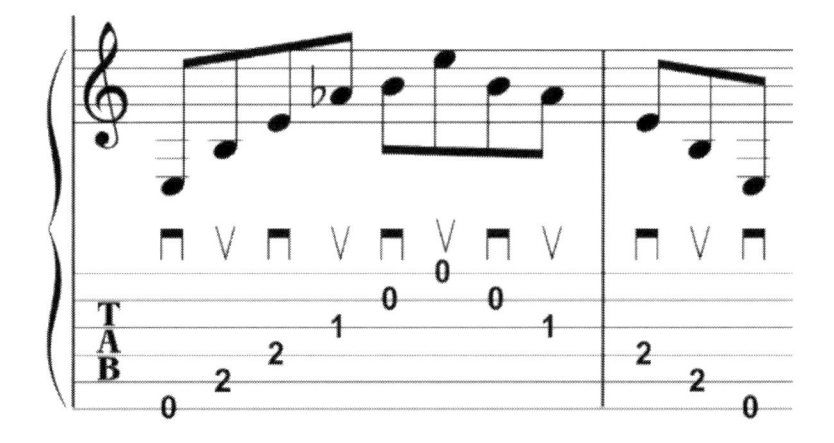

You can do this exercise with any chords you want, including 4 and 5 note shapes. The number of strings will change the right hand feel, so change it up!

This is a powerful exercise for building good right hand picking technique. It also helps take away the awkwardness many guitarists feel when playing upstrokes.

For a more advanced workout, throw some string skipping into it like this:

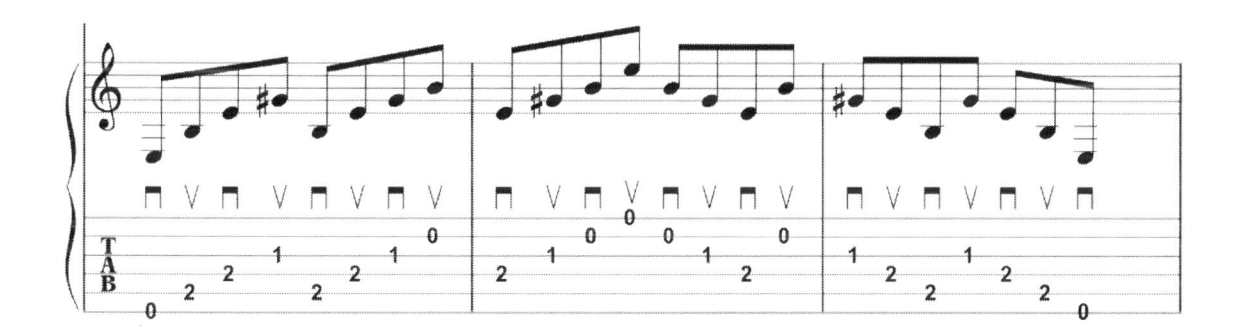

I've taken this string skipping pattern and applied it to Heitor Villa-Lobos famous Etude #1 for an incredible chord and picking workout. This is my absolute go-to exercise when my picking hand is feeling a little "off".

Note: This thing is a monster on both hands, so go easy. Work through it slow and build it up gradually.

VILLA-LOBOS PICKING STUDY

Heitor Villa-Lobos (1887-1959) was a Brazilian composer, conductor, cellist, pianist, and guitarist. Villa-Lobos was described as "the single most significant creative figure in 20th-century Brazilian art music". Villa-Lobos has become the best-known South American composer of all time. A prolific composer, he wrote numerous orchestral, chamber, instrumental and vocal works, totaling over 2000 works by his death in 1959.

His Etudes for guitar (1929) were dedicated to Andrés Segovia. The 12 Etudes remain one of the most important works in the solo classical guitar repertoire.

Here we're going to take an excerpt from Villa-Lobos' famous Etude #1 and arrange it for alternate picking. If you'd like to try the original Classical Guitar fingered Etudes or any of his other Solo Guitar Works you can pick them up on Amazon here.

Even though you could achieve the same results by just doing this picking pattern in any 6 string chord, I think it feels better to play an actual piece of music.

It's nice to have a beginning and end to any exercise. As daunting as this looks, it really only takes a few minutes to get through once you have the chords memorized.

If you really get one thing out of this book, make it this one! To my knowledge this has never been adapted to pick-style technique. I came up with the idea for this about 10 years ago and it has helped my alternate picking so much.

This has been the single most most effective picking exercise I've ever learned, and it's just a great sounding piece of music.

Villa-Lobos Etude:

Villa-Lobos Picking Etude
Arr. Craig Smith

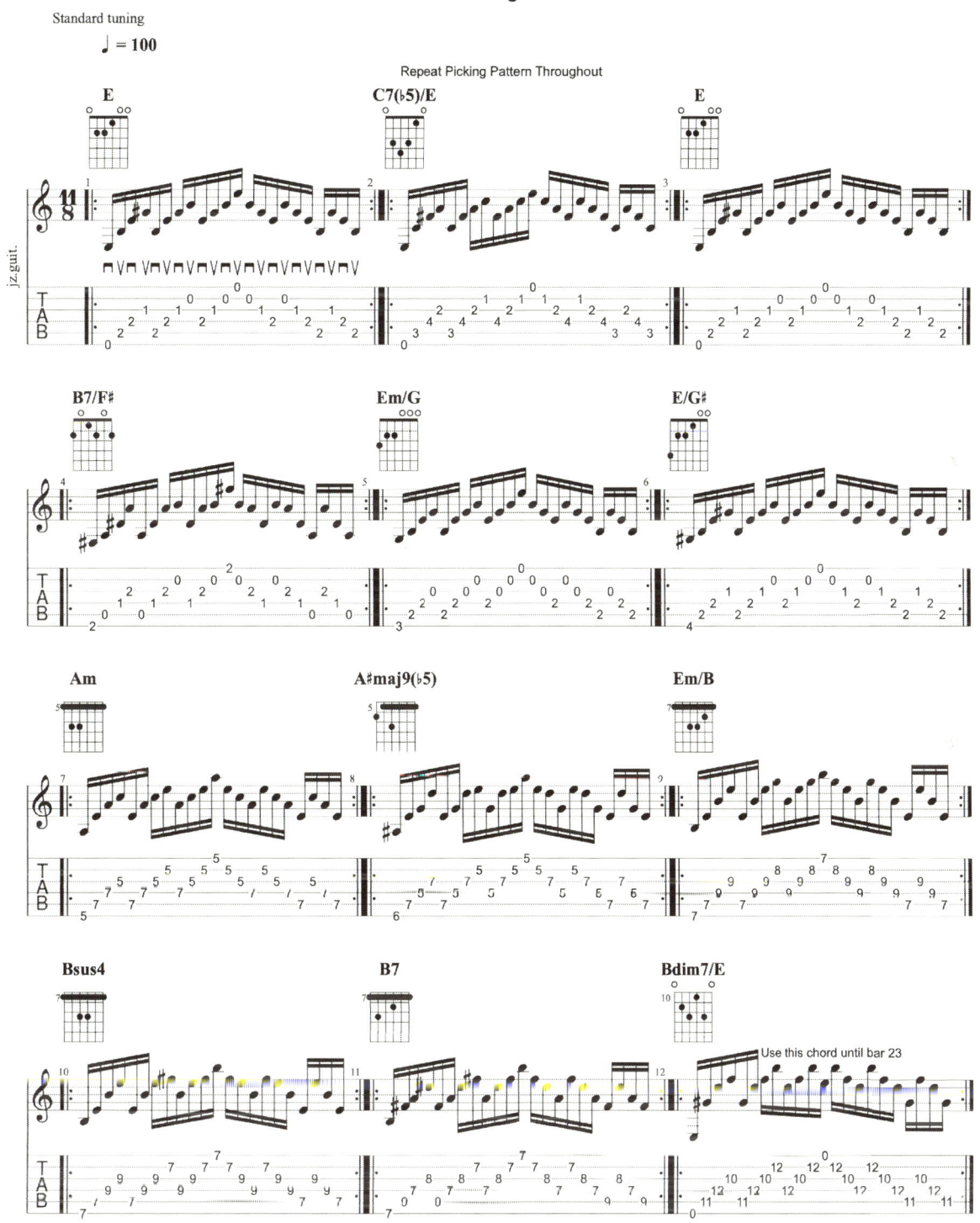

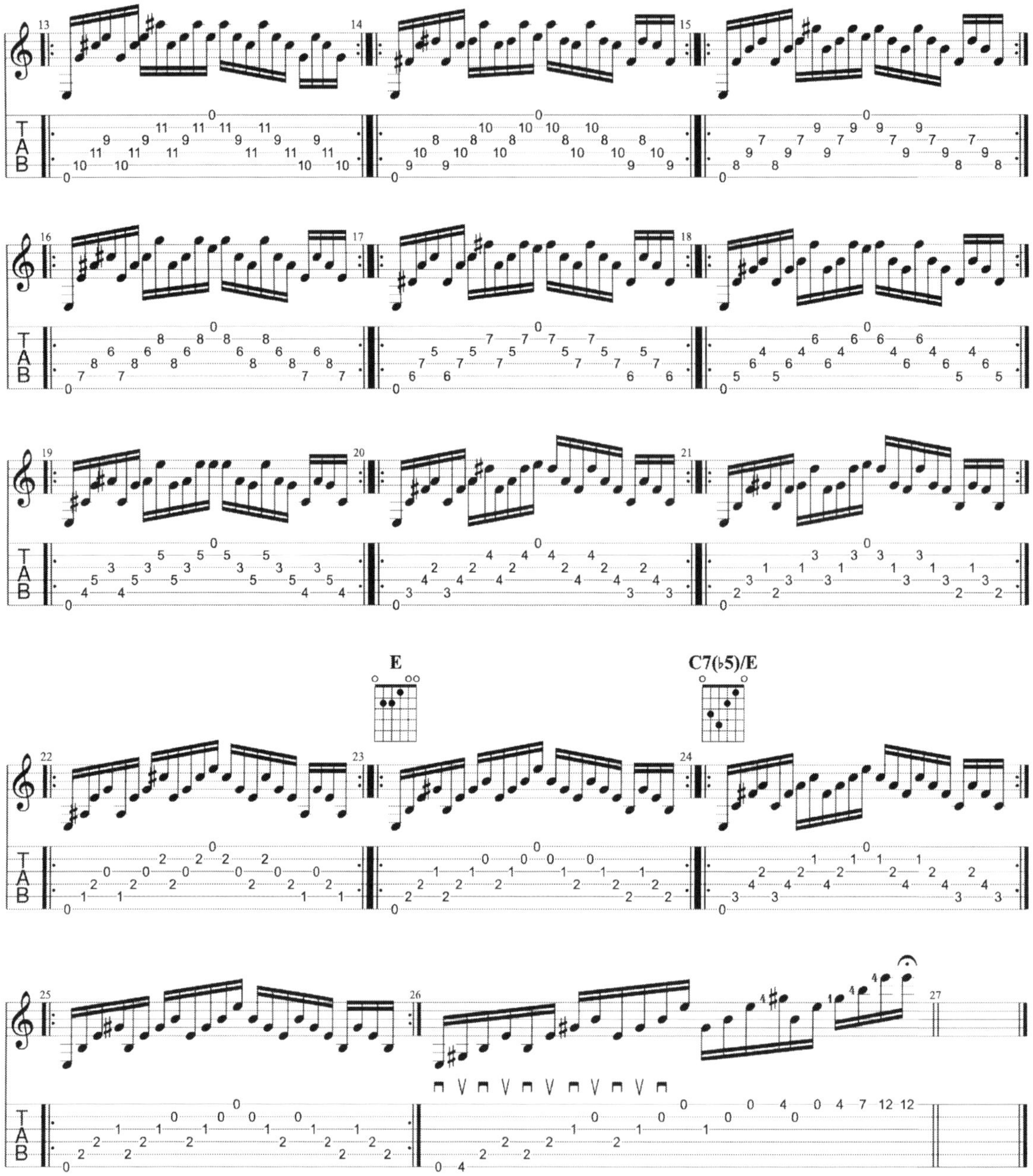
E
C7(♭5)/E

DOUBLE-TRIPLETS WITH SPEED BURSTS

Lastly, we're going to change it up yet again by going to single string only sequences.

These really help keep my picking in shape. They're also very helpful with improving the synchronization between hands.

For this example, I'm using the G Major Scale (**G A B C D E F# G**) starting on the first string using the first available fretted note in the scale (F#) in the second position.

- *Find a comfortable speed to play the first 4 triplets before double-timing it for the last two.*
- *Continue on up the neck diatonically in G Major. The next set would be G, A, B, then A, B, C, etc. until you run out of frets.*
- *Flip it around by starting on your pinky and do them in reverse. A, G, F# then B, A, G etc. You can do them on just one string or all 6, just stay in key.*
- *I also like to tweak this by playing the first 4 triplets in 4/4, then switch to a fast blast of 6/8 feel for the last 2. Whatever works for you. Have fun with it!*
- *Do a different key every Monday.* **This is really important**. *The more different keys you practice in the better for your overall improvisation.*

Below I've written them ascending on the high E, descending on the B string with speed bursts. *Do as many as you have time for today.*

Double Triplet Example:

Double Triplets
Speed Bursts

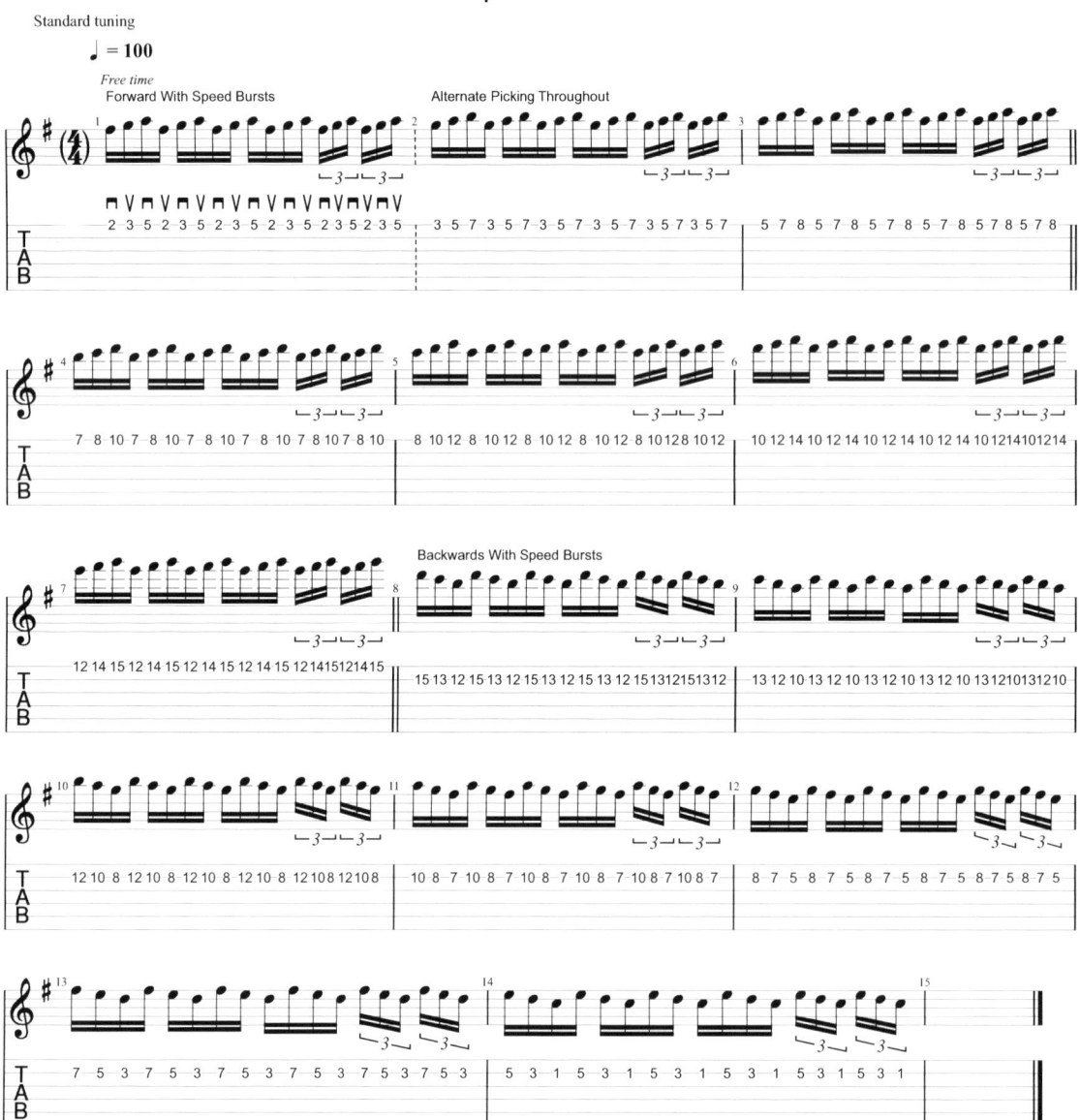

MONDAY ROUTINE ROUNDUP

1. *2 Sets of 4-Note-Per String combos to 12th position and back.*

2. *Alternate pick through open chords or do the Villa-Lobos study (advanced).*

3. *Double Triplets on all 6 strings, forward and backward.*

TUESDAY - THE MODAL WORKOUT

Tuesday's routine is a bit more involved and includes a Modal Scale Workout. This exercise utilizes each of the 7 Diatonic Modal shapes, alternate picking variations, legato and arpeggios.

If you're new to modes, or do not yet have the shapes memorized, hopefully this lesson will take some of the mystery out of it.

WHAT IS A MODE?

The easiest *(or simplest)* way to think of a mode is to just think of each mode as a new scale built on a degree of an existing scale.

For example, a G Major Scale consists of these notes:
G A B C D E F# G

The first Diatonic mode Ionian, is synonymous with a Major Scale. You could call the above scale G Major or G Ionian.

To build the next mode, simply start on the next note (A) and build a new scale:
A B C D E F# G A - (notice I didn't change any notes)

We now have A Dorian.

Starting on the next note (B) we can build B Phrygian:
B C D E F# G A B (same notes, just starting on B)

We didn't change the notes, we just built a new scale on each subsequent note. A Dorian is not an A Major scale (A B C# D E F# G# A). It is simply a G Major scale starting on the second degree (A).

You could think of A Dorian as an A Major Scale with a b3 and b7, or just think of it as the second mode (ii minor) in G Major.

How you visualize what a mode is in relation to what you're using it for will determine whether you think of it as relating to the key of (A) or just a mode of G Major.

For example, if I'm playing over a simple A minor chord vamp, I could theoretically play any A minor type scale or mode such as A minor Pentatonic, A Dorian, A Phrygian, A Aeolian etc, al.

The flip side to that example is, I can also play any OTHER mode in G Major over that same A minor chord vamp.

Why does that work?

- A minor is the ii minor chord in G Major.
- All of the notes in an A minor chord (A C E) exist within the G Major scale.
- Therefore, the G Major scale covers all of the notes in the A minor chord (and then some). G **A** B **C** D **E** F# G

The Key Center Approach

For the purposes of this book I'm going to use Modal Scales using a "Key Center" approach. This essentially breaks up the guitar neck into 7 Modes per Major Key. All 7 Modes will be in the same Key and played on their respective root notes of each scale degree.

Modes in the Key of G Major:

I. G Ionian
II. A Dorian
III. B Phrygian
IV. C Lydian
V. D Mixolydian
VI. E Aeolian
VII. F# Locrian

When I'm using the "Key Center Approach", I tend to think of them less as individual modes *(with specific sounds and characteristics)*, and just part of the parent Key of G Major.

This is the easiest way to digest modal playing if you're not already intimately familiar with using modal scales.

3 NOTE-PER-STRING MODES

Using 3 Note-Per-String Modal shapes, you get a nice overlap between each mode which helps visualize where the "good notes" are when improvising or writing a song or solo.

Ionian overlaps Dorian. Dorian overlaps Phrygian and so on. A good way to use this overlap visualization is to improvise over a backing track using only 1 or 2 adjacent modes such as G Ionian and A Dorian. when this becomes comfortable, move on to the next pair.

If you're completely new to modes I've included a printable page below with all 7 shapes. For the rest of you, move on to the workout!

MODAL SHAPES

Ionian

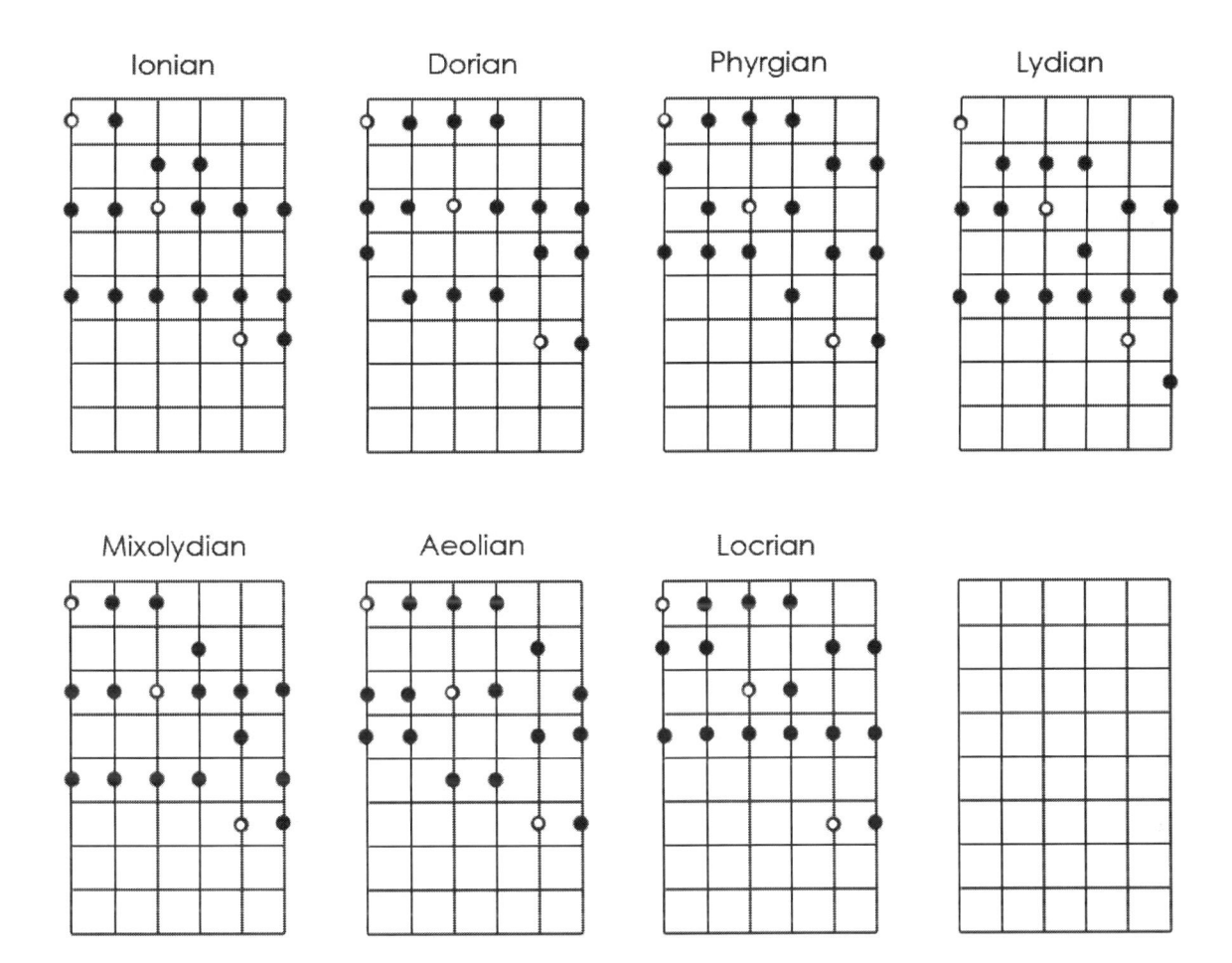

Dorian

Phyrgian

Lydian

Mixolydian

Aeolian

Locrian

THE MODAL WORKOUT

This workout can be thought of in separate sequences or variations using each modal shape:

- **Regular** - Ascending and descending using alternate picking.
- **3rds** - 1-3-2-4-3-5-4-6 etc.
- **4's** - 1234, 2345, 3456, 4567 etc.
- **Up & Back** - A variation that exploits the difficulty of the upstroke on adjacent strings.
- **Arpeggios** - *Yes!* There are diatonic arpeggios hidden in each modal shape.
- **Legato** - Hammer-on and pull-off variations best suited for electric guitarists.

Tips on Practicing the Workout:

- *Memorize all the sequences in Ionian until they are comfortable and can be played without mistakes (and without stopping).*
- *Take a break after every 1-2 modes.*
- *If it hurts, STOP. Never play through pain.*
- *Always use a metronome! If you don't have one, they're cheap. Grab one on Amazon or at your local music shop.*
- *Allocate enough time to do the workout in all 7 modes.*
- *At 100 BPM the entire workout takes about 40 minutes.*
- *Always alternate your pick strokes. Keep an eye on that right hand.*
- *Practice slow at first. Never practice faster than you can play **perfectly**.*

The Regular Sequence

Straight alternate picking ascending and descending. I like to do this 4-10 times to warm up before moving into the 3rds sequence depending on how much time I have. In the music example below, it's played only once.

```
|-------------------------------5-----7-8-7-5-----------------|
|-------------------5--7--8-------------------8-7-5-----------|
|-------------4-5-7-------------------------------7-5-4-------|
|-------3-5-7---------------------------------------------7-5-4----|
|-3-5-7---------------------------------------------------------7-5-3--|
|---------------------------------------------------------------------7-5-3|
```

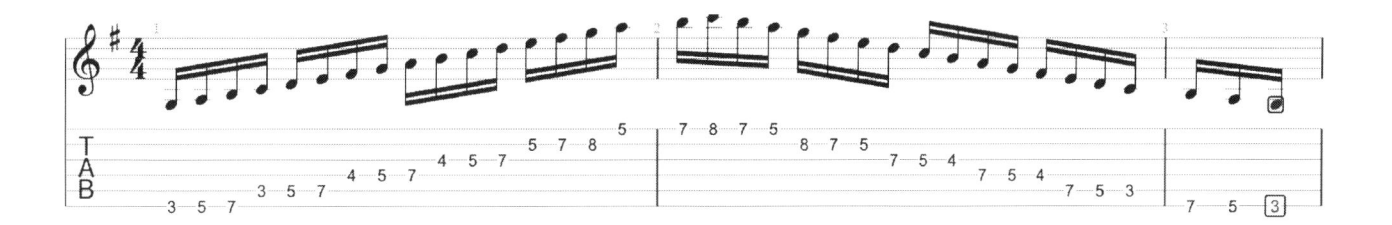

Go right into the "3rds" and "4's" sequences without stopping. You're going to continue into each sequence without stopping or changing your alternate picking. Always alternate pick throughout the workout.

3rds Sequence:

For 3rds you're just playing up 2, back one, etc. 1st, 3rd, 2nd, 4th... Like this:

∏ V ∏ V

```
|-----------------------------------------------------5-----7-5-8|
|-------------------------------------------5---7-5-8---8--------|
|-----------------------------4-----5-4-7-5---7------------------|
|-------------3-----5-3-7-5-----5-4-7--------7-------------------|
|-3-7-5---5-7----------7---------------------------------------- |
|-----7-----------------------------------------------------------|
```

Fours

For "Fours", we're going to play 1-2-3-4, 2-3-4-5, 3-4-5-6 etc.

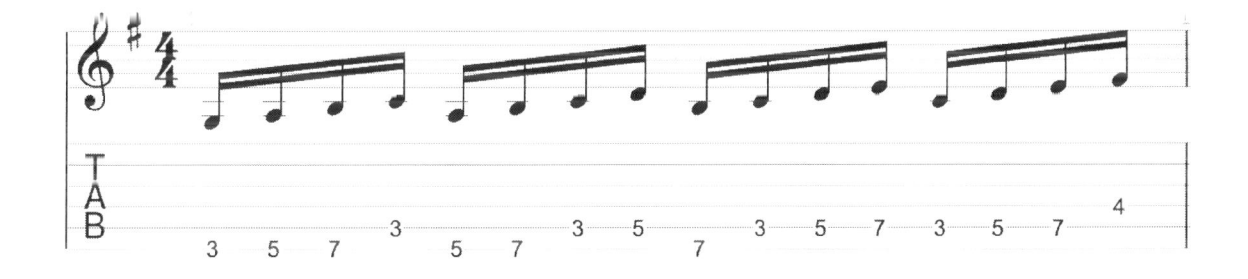

```
|-----------------------------------------------------------4-|
|-------------------------------------3---5---7---3---5---7---|
|-------------------3---5---7---3---5---7---------------------|
|-3---5---7---3---5---7---------------------------------------|
```

The "Up & Back"

The "Up & Back" sequence is a variation on an old Paul Gilbert exercise he used to teach at G.I.T. in the 1980's. Here's an example:

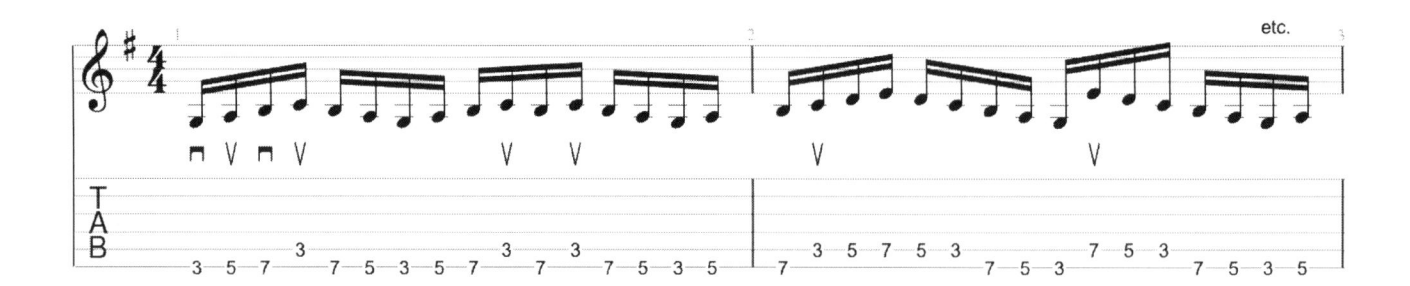

```
    3-5-7     3         3         3      3-5-7-5-3    7-5-3
          7-5-3-5-7   7   7-5-3-5          7              7-5-3-5
```
(⊓ V ⊓ V   V   V   V   V   etc.)

The funny thing is, he got it from Al Di Meola who had done this exact sequence as far back as 1975.

You can hear a pristinely executed example of this on the live album Friday Night in San Francisco track "Mediterranean Sundance/Rio Ancho". *A Must own for any guitarist.*

Regardless of who did it first, it's a wonderful exercise that focuses on the difficult "outside picking" problem.

When you pick on a downstroke on one string, and an upstroke on the next higher adjacent string, it's called "Outside Picking".

There are a lot of ways you can do the "Up & Back". Feel free to experiment and tweak it to help any deficiencies in your picking technique.

DIATONIC ARPEGGIOS INSIDE MODES

Even if you've been blazing these modes for years, you may not have noticed the hidden arpeggios in each shape.

Each modal shape contains diatonic 7th arpeggios that can be used for a variety of improvising applications. These arpeggios will give your solos a more focused and sophisticated sound. They also make for an excellent picking workout that involves some string skipping.

It's also a beautiful thing when you can make a scale *not* sound like a scale. This sequence is wonderful for that.

The Diatonic 7th Arpeggios/Chords in the Key of G Major are:

I. G Major 7 - GBDF#
II. A minor 7 - ACEG
III. B minor 7 - BDF#A
IV. C Major 7   CEGB
V. D Dominant 7 - DF#AC
VI. E minor 7 - EGBD
VII. F# minor 7b5 - F#ACE

These arpeggios are hidden in all of the 7 modal shapes.
As with the rest of the sequences, I sometimes will tweak this to include extra repeats. This one is probably my favorite sequence, and a lot of fun!

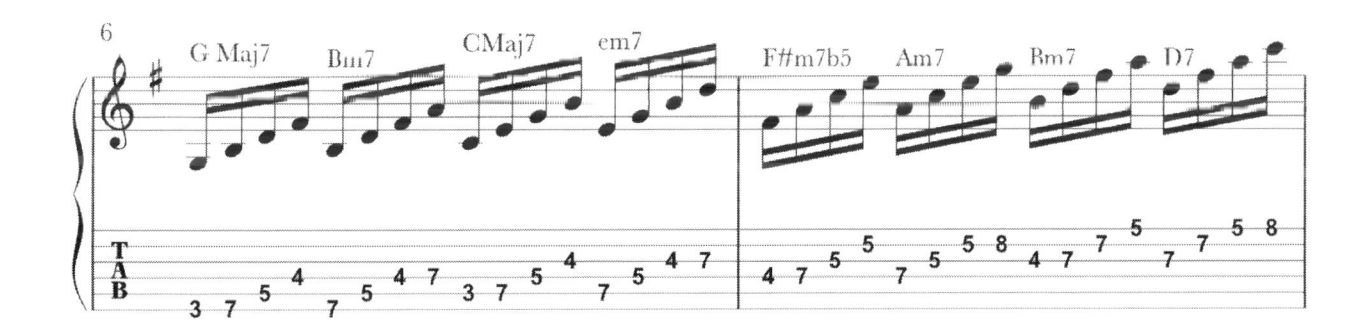

The Legato Sequence

The last part of the Modal Workout should be pretty self-explanatory. We're going to give the left hand a little love on this one. You could do this sequence on the acoustic guitar but it's much better suited for electric playing styles.

Legato Defined: "In a smooth flowing manner, without breaks."

Starting on a downstroke you'll then slur *(hammer-on)* each subsequent scale tone with the left hand on the low E string. When moving to the A string you'll use an upstroke and repeat. On the high-E you will slur the turnaround without changing the picking.

Remember:
- *Always alternate your picking strokes!*
- *No breaks between notes. Legato should be one continuously flowing line of notes.*

Example:

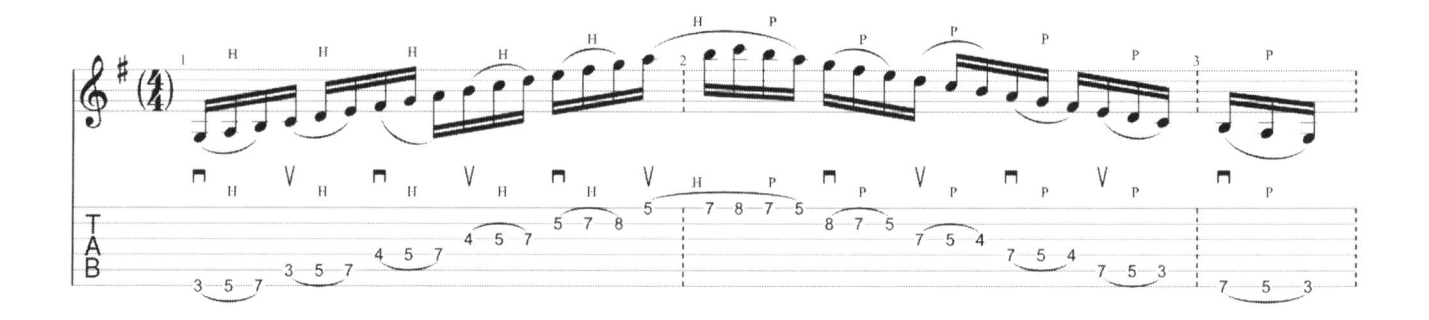

THE MODAL WORKOUT

Putting it all together:

The Modal Workout
G Ionian

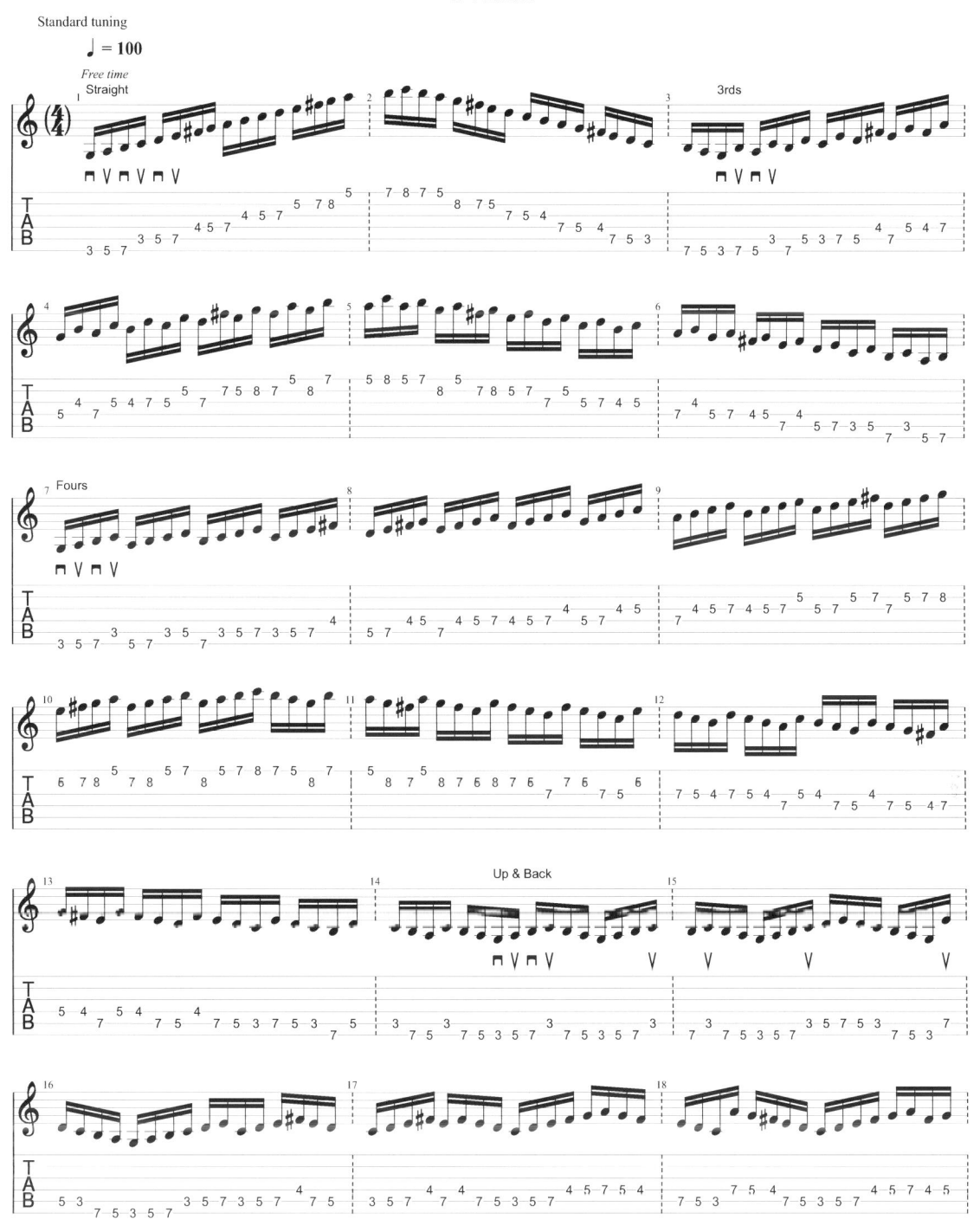

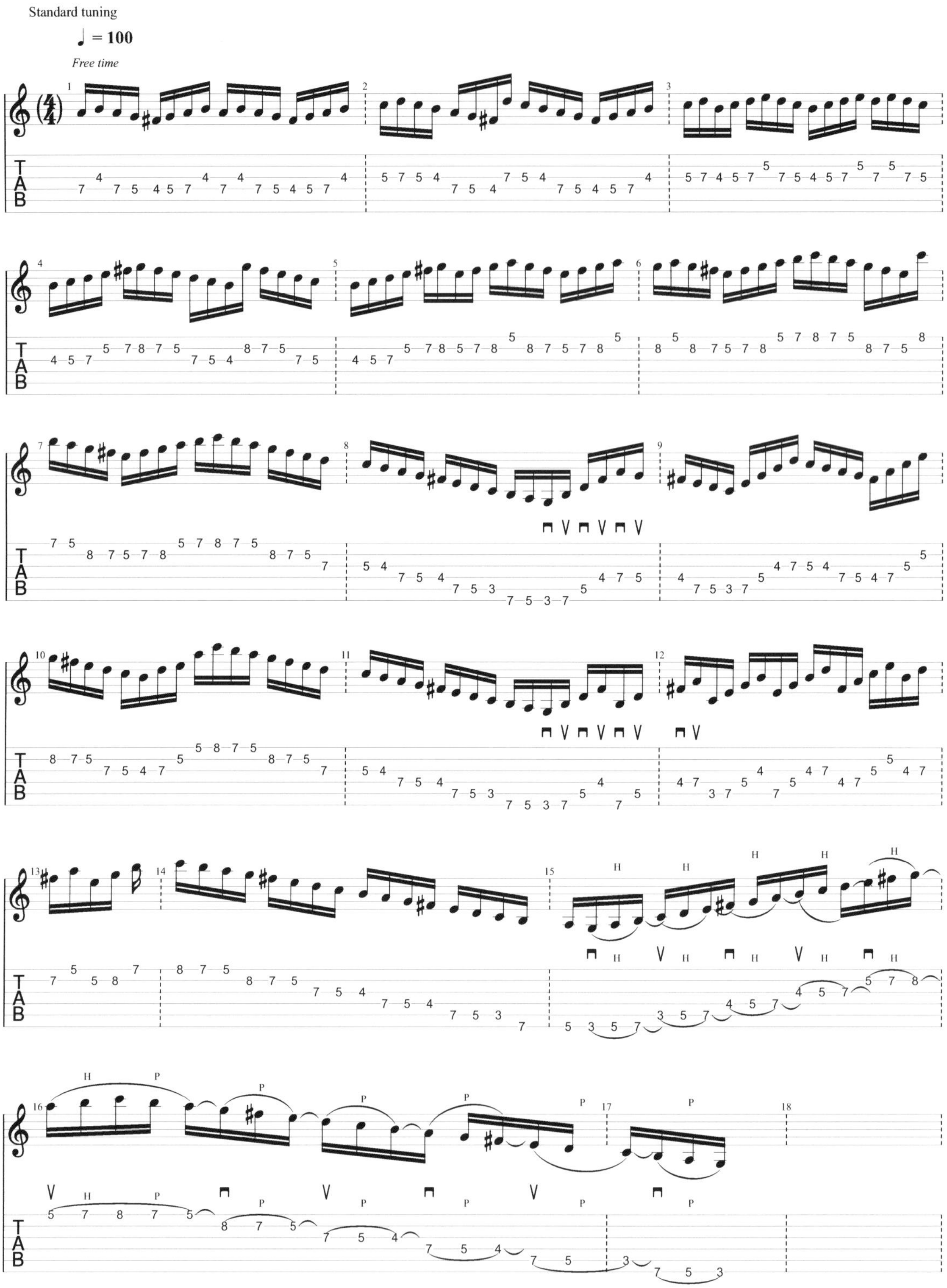
Standard tuning
♩ = 100
Free time

TUESDAY ROUTINE ROUNDUP

- *Work on each sequence separately until it feels comfortable at a slow speed.*
- *Memorize the entire sequence in G Ionian.*
- *Repeat the entire Modal Workout using the other modes: Dorian, Phrygian, Lydian, Mixolydian, Aeolian and Locrian.*
- *Try it in a different Key each week.*

WEDNESDAY - ARPEGGIOS

Diatonic Triads - G String Root

Before we get into the big & meaty arpeggio shapes, we're going to start off with some simple triads. This lesson will be in the key of C Major/A minor.

If you're a beginner or even a more advanced player not familiar with these shapes, take a strum through them first without the picking sequences.

Diatonic Chords & Arpeggios in C Major:

I.   C Major - CEG
II. D minor - DFA
III. E minor - EGB
IV. F Major - FAC
V.   G Major - GBD
VI. A minor - ACE
VII. B diminished - BDF

TRIADS

Starting in the 2nd position with A minor, we're going to do a simple ascending/descending alternate picking sequence through all of the arpeggios.

This first set will only include triads with the root notes on the G String:

- **Set #1** - Alternate pick through the triads starting on the A note *(2nd fret, G String)*, and continue through all of the arpeggios up the neck.
- If these triads feel even a little uncomfortable, go ahead and repeat each one 2-4x before switching to the next one.

- **Set #2** - In an ascending triplet feel were changing the picking to - DOWN, DOWN, UP.
- **Set #3** - In a descending triplet feel, switch to - UP, UP, DOWN.
- **Set # 4** - "Double-pick" each note in each arpeggio ascending and descending.

Below is an example using the first few arpeggios in C Major:

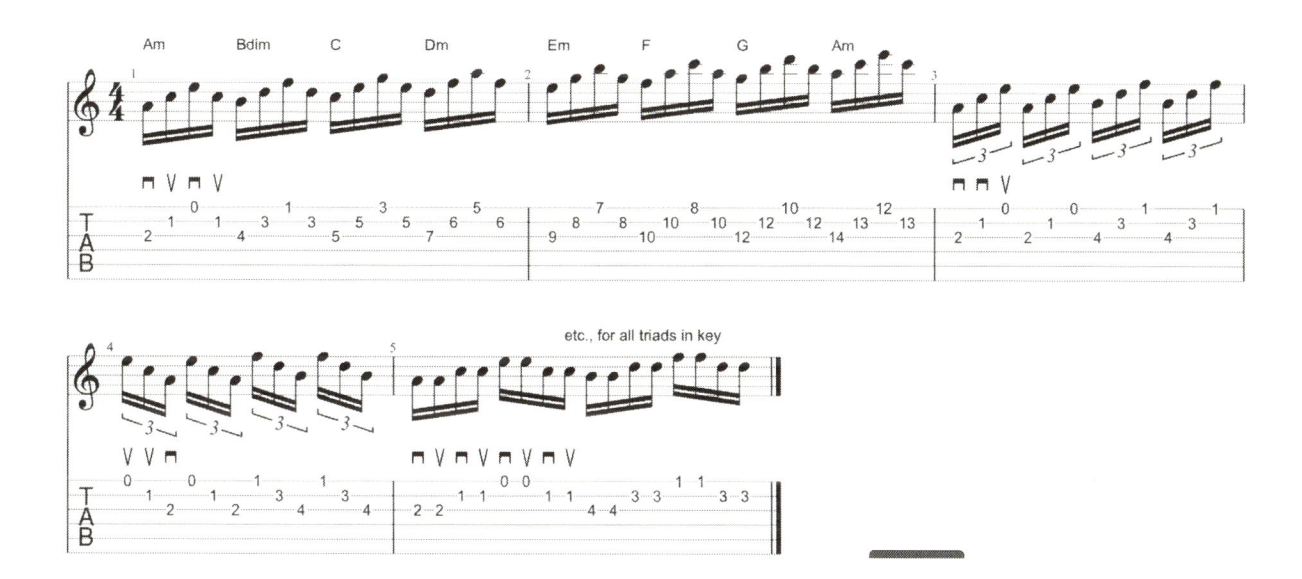

Diatonic Triads - D, A & E String Roots

You can probably see where I'm going with this right? We're going to do the exact same 4 sets, but move the triads "down" to the D string shapes.

- *Starting on the E note (2nd fret, D String), build your arpeggios diatonically up the neck in the key of C Major.*
- *Do the same thing starting on the B (2nd fret, A string) and the G (3rd fret, low E string).*

For the purposes of this book I'll avoid the redundancy of putting all that repetitive music here.

5 STRING DIATONIC ARPEGGIOS

Sweep picking big 5 string arpeggios shapes greatly benefits your fretting hand strength and dexterity. The exercises below will benefit both hands greatly. Just don't overuse it.

This first set consists of an A String root, 1 note per string except for 2 notes on the high E. These are the most common arpeggio shapes.

G Major - This shape can be used for the I, IV and V degrees: C, F & G Major

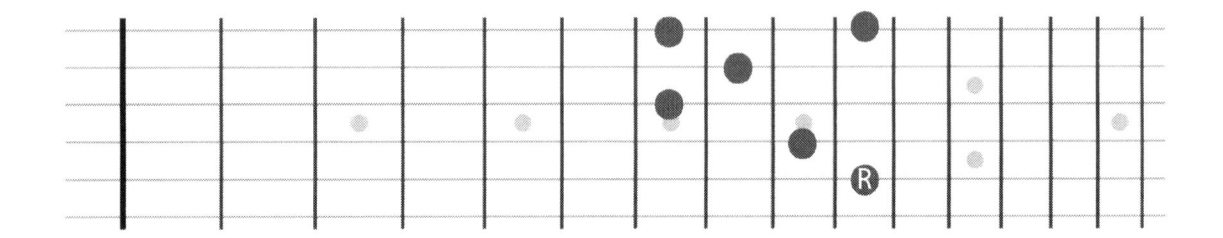

Am - This shape can be used for the ii, iii and vi degrees of the scale: D, E & A minor.

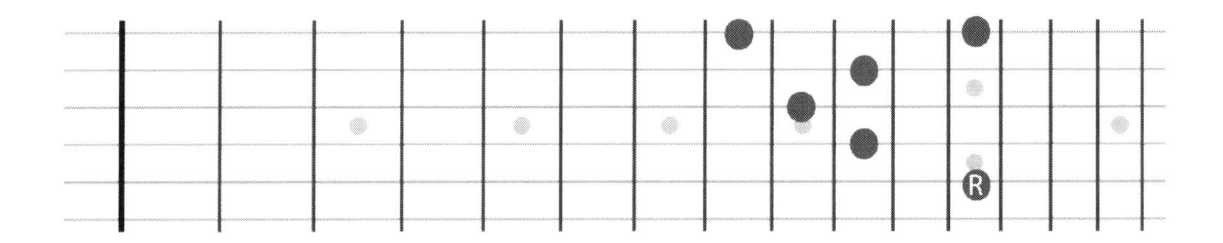

B Diminished. This shape can be used for the vii.

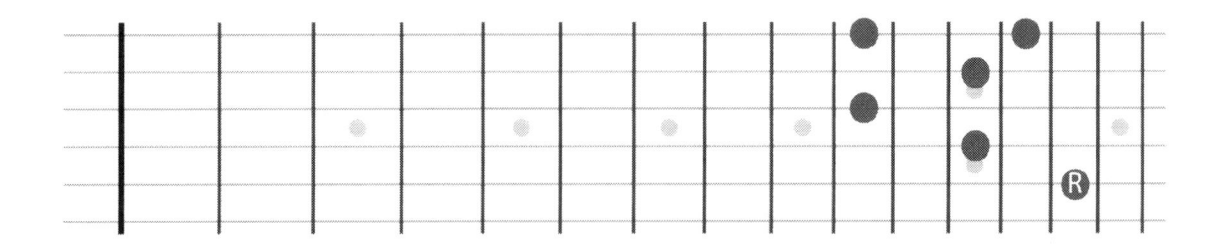

The real challenge here is the picking. It's tricky but worth the effort!

Once you're comfortable with the shapes, here's a sequence utilizing more arpeggios in the Key of C Major.

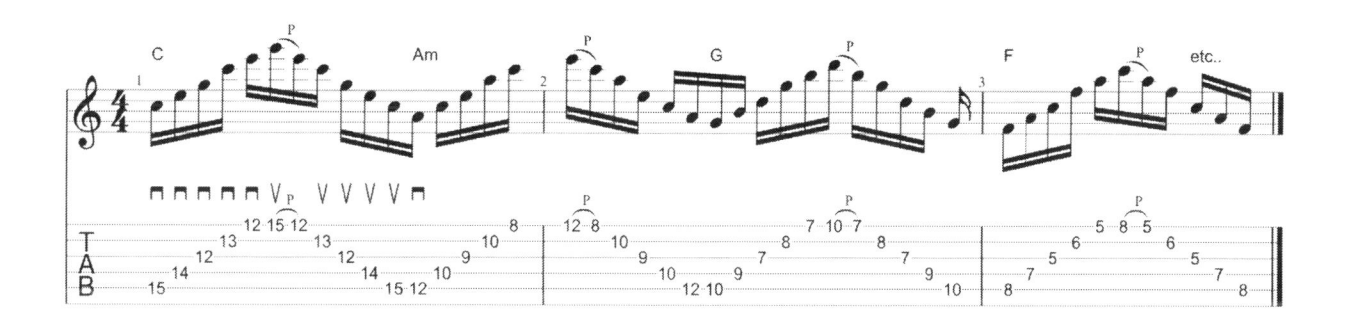

For the next one, I like to add an extra low note *(the 5th)* on the A string to each arpeggio. This gives it a nice flow for playing them in time with a 16th *(or 32nd)* note feel.

For example if we take the G Major shape from above and add a low 5th played with the first finger, it looks like this:

It looks like a scary stretch, but you'll get it with slow practice.

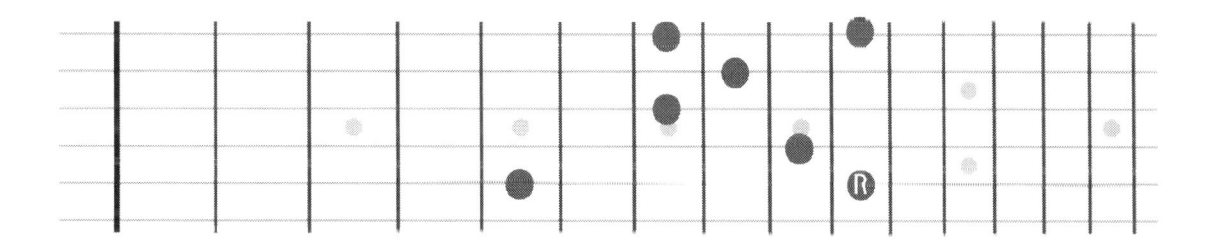

Here's a few more using this extra low 5th pattern:

You can tweak this out any way you like. They are a lot of fun, so happy shredding!

ARPEGGIO WORKOUT

Arpeggio Study
Key of C Major

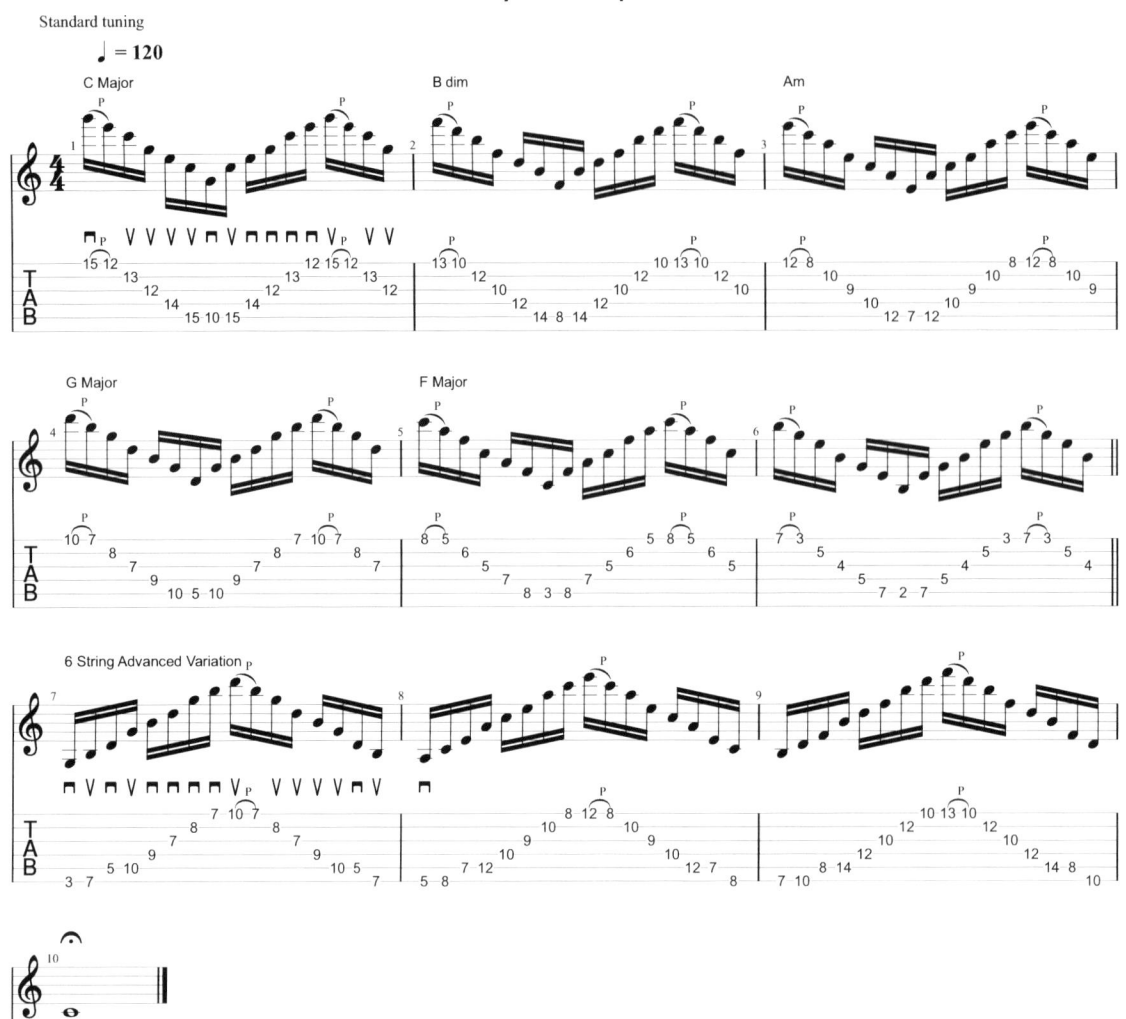

DIATONIC 7TH ARPEGGIOS

These are really the meat & potatoes of my improvising tools. Along with Modal scales, Diatonic 7th Arpeggios provide an excellent framework for improvising in just about any music style.

They can sound a little jazzy or a little shreddy. Some even sound Bluesy. They just work everywhere and will give your solos a really sophisticated and focused sound. They sound cool without the cheesy "shred" stigma, *(in case you're trying to avoid that.)*

All we're doing here is adding that 7th scale degree to the existing (1,3,5) arpeggios we did above. If it helps to make the association with modes, that's fine, whatever works for you.

You could think of it like this:

I. C Ionian: C D E F G A B C ——> **C Major 7**
II. D Dorian: D E F G A B C D ——> **D minor 7**
III. E Phrygian: E F G A B C D E ——>**E minor 7**
IV. F Lydian: F G A B C D E F ——-> **F Major 7**
V. G Mixolydian: G A B C D E F G ——-> **G Dominant 7**
VI. A Aeolian: A B C D E F G A ——-> **A minor 7**
VII. B Locrian: B C D E F G A B > **B minor 7b5**

7TH ARPEGGIO SHAPES:

I find it easier to memorize these in different places by thinking of a *"behind the root"* and *"in front of the root"* shape.

Here's a CMaj7 "Behind the Root" shape:

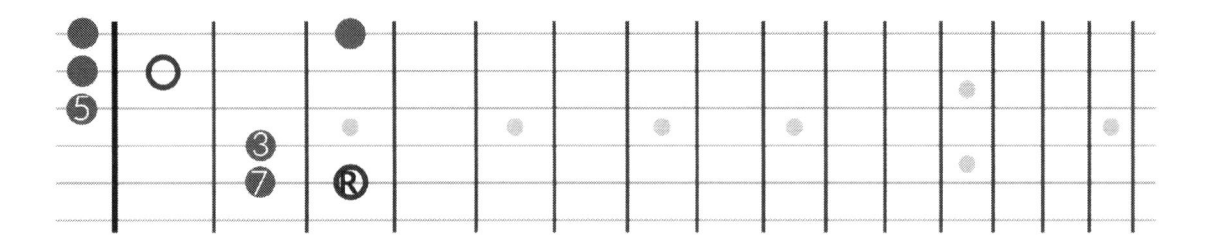

You can also use this shape for the **IV: FMaj7**. Just move the root to the F note on the 8th fret, A String.

We could map out an almost infinite number of arpeggio shapes for each degree in the scale, but for the sake of this exercise, let's work on just 1 for each scale degree.

ii Dm7, iii Em7 and vi Am7 can all use this shape:

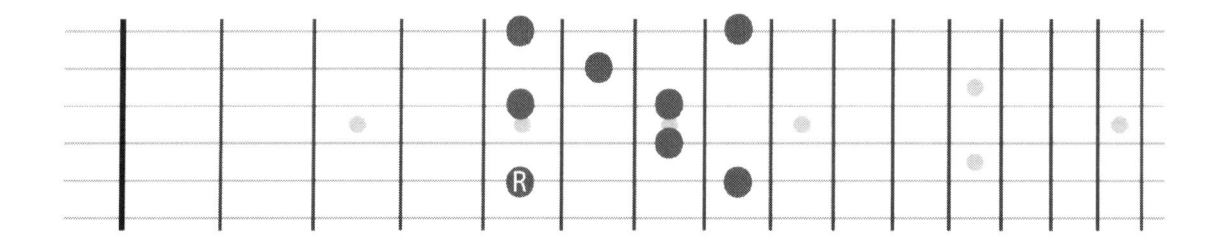

Dm7 can be played (above) in the 5th position. Em7 in the 7th position and Am7 in the open or 12th position.

V - G7

Remember that the V-chord is a 1-3-5-b7. This will warrant a new shape for G7:

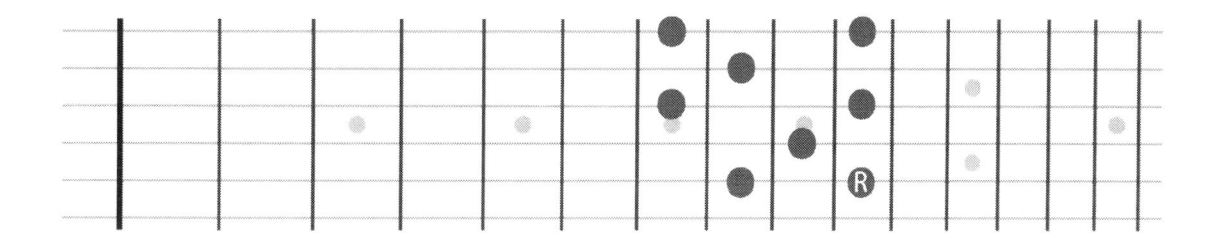

vii - Bm7b5

The vii chord in every key is a minor7b5:

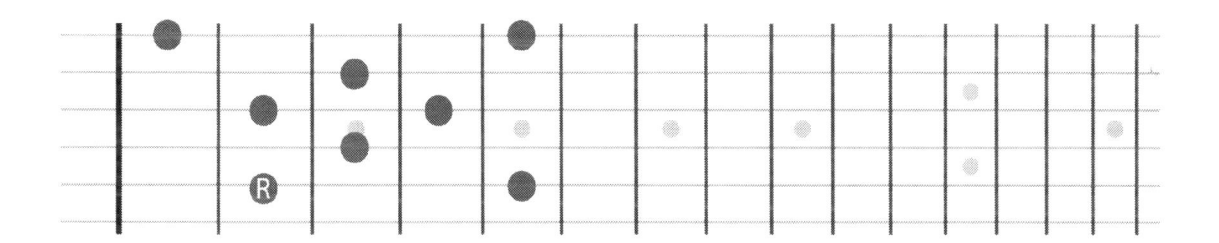

Using Dm7 as an example: Starting on the 5th fret (D note) alternate pick ascending through the arpeggio and continue alternate picking descending, like this:

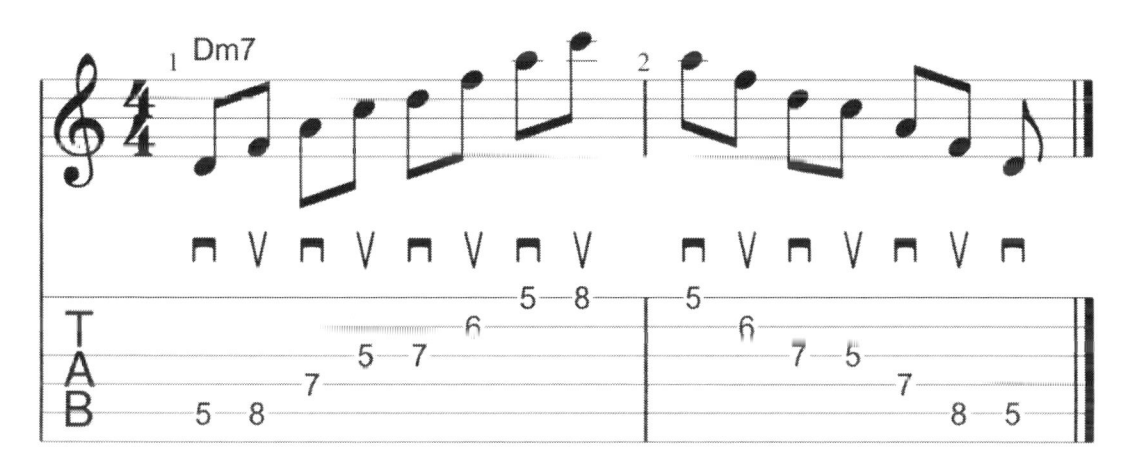

Some Usage and Analysis:

7th arpeggios can give you a wide array of sounds. You can play them with a Key Center approach by just mixing and matching sequences you like. They ALL work in the key regardless of what the chord progression is *(assuming the chords are in the Key too)*.

You can also use them for a more focused sound. For example, playing an Am7 arpeggio over a Dm7 chord, gives you a D minor 11th sound. Jazzy right? ***Why you ask?***

Am7 = ACEG

In relation to D those notes would be thought of as:
A - 5th of D
C - b7 of D
E - 2nd or 9th of D
G - 4th or 11th of D

With this type of approach you're kind of forcing the listener into a certain sound by superimposing one chord/arpeggio over another in the same key.

You can go nuts with that little nugget of info and try different combos that sound good to you.

More Tips For Memorizing Arpeggios:

Think of the lines and spaces on the Treble Clef when memorizing the notes in arpeggios. For example, the spaces in standard music notation are:
F-A-C-E... Hey, thats an F Major 7! *(Mind Blown)*

The Treble Clef lines starting on E:
Remember that saying when you were a kid?
EVERY GOOD BOY DOES FINE

Every Good Boy:

E-G-B = Em

Every Good Boy Does:

E-G-B-D = Em7

Every Good Boy Does Fine:

E-G-B-D-F = Em9

Pretty cool right? I know it helps me in times of doubt.

WEDNESDAY ROUTINE ROUNDUP

- *Beginners:* Learn at least 1 new arpeggio shape every Wednesday
- *Advanced:* Play through each arpeggio, workout and sequence 10x in a different key each week.

THURSDAY - SCALES

Today we're going to focus on something a little obvious. *Scales*. I know it can be a daunting and often boring part of your guitar practice routine, but seriously, Scales need some love too and they can be super fun!

WHAT IS A SCALE?

By definition, "In music theory, a scale is any set of musical notes ordered by fundamental frequency or pitch. A scale ordered by increasing pitch is an ascending scale, and a scale ordered by decreasing pitch is a descending scale"

Or in lay terms, alphabetically from A to G. For example the C Major Scale:

C D E F G A B C

The Major scale is the foundation for all other scales, chords arpeggios.. really anything you're going to do on the Guitar *(or any other instrument)*.

The Major Scale:

- A Major Scale has 8 notes in alphabetical order.
- Has a set interval pattern, (the space between scale tones) for every key:

Whole, Whole, Half, Whole, Whole, Whole, Half

If you're completely new to music theory, think of a whole step as 2 frets distance on the guitar and a half step as 1 fret.

There are always half steps between the notes B-C and E-F.

Circle of Keys

THE CIRCLE OF KEYS:

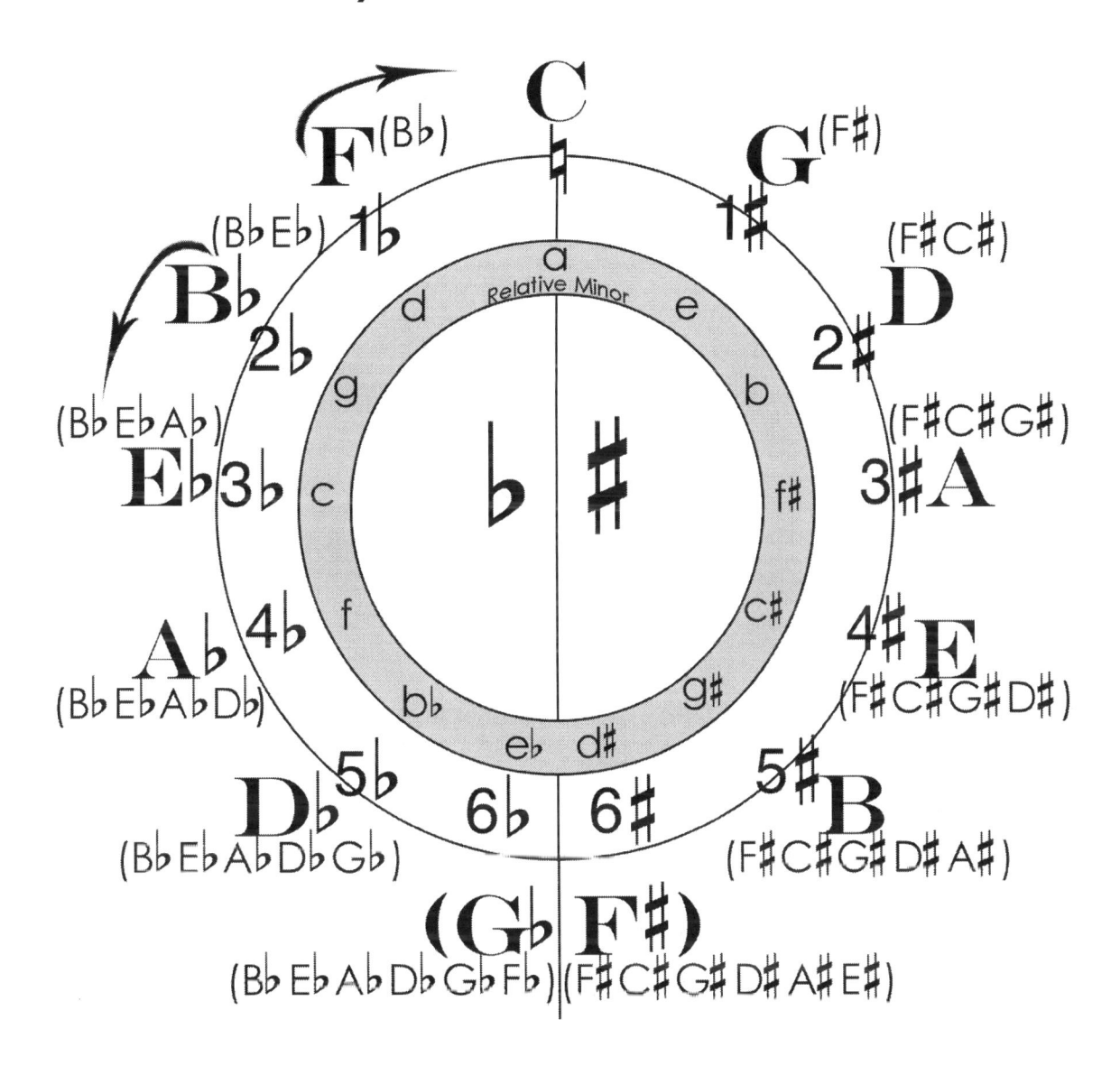

The Circle of Keys *(often called the Circle of 5ths)* is a kind of calculator to determine the notes in any Major Scale.

The Major Scale consists of 7 different notes and one octave note in alphabetical order. For example a C Major Scale is simply: C D E F G A B C

The formula for a Major Scale is:
Whole, Whole, Half, Whole, Whole, Whole, Half

Remember that a whole step *(Whole Tone)* is equal to 2 frets distance, while a half-step *(Semi-Tone)* equals only 1 frets distance.

With this knowledge you could build a Major Scale off of any note, providing you stick with the above formula.

When you apply this formula starting on the note C proceeding through the musical alphabet you can see how this works:

I.   C to D is a Whole Step.
II. D to E is a Whole step
III. E to F is a Half-Step
IV. F to G is a Whole Step
V.   G to A is a Whole Step
VI. A to B is a Whole Step
VII. B to C (octave) is a Half -Step

Being able to figure out scales in this manner is a valuable tool that can be applied to any instrument. For the guitar, it is a slow process that can be averted by the use of patterns and modes.

How the Circle Works:

THE SHARP SIDE

Starting at the top of the circle with the Key of C Major, notice the natural sign indicating a key signature of **NO sharps and NO Flats**.

This means that if we start a scale on "C" ascending in alphabetical order, we end up with **C D E F G A B C** without having to change anything.

As we travel clockwise in 5th's to the next note "G", we add 1 sharp note.
The first sharp note is F#, indicated by the arrow pointing clockwise.
After we add the F# we end up with a **G Major Scale: G A B C D E F# G.**

Continuing on to the next key clockwise, we get the key of D Major.
D Major contains 2 sharp notes, F# and C#.
Remember when we need to add a sharp, start on F#, then follow the arrow clockwise and add the next one in 5ths.

We end up with **D E F# G A B C# D**.

Try playing these notes on the guitar and notice how our Major Scale Formula remains intact.

Proceeding to our next Key, A Major we add another sharp for a total of 3.
Starting on F#, following the arrow clockwise and adding C# and D#.

A Major Scale: A B C# D E F# G# A

Can you see the pattern forming here?

Some Important Points to Remember:

- *The Major scales always contain 8 notes in alphabetical order.*
- *We always start on F when adding sharps and then add additional ones in 5ths, or clockwise following the arrow.*
- *The finished product ALWAYS falls into our Major Scale Formula:* **Whole, Whole, Half, Whole, Whole, Whole, Half.**

THE FLAT SIDE

We build "flat" Keys in much the same way that we did with the sharp side of the circle, but with two important differences:

1. Bb is the first flat note.
2. We add our flat notes counter-clockwise (in 4ths) indicated by the arrow above Bb.

For the key of F Major, we add 1 flat note.
The first flat note is Bb.
So our F Major Scale looks like this: **F G A Bb C D E F**

Our second flat KEY "Bb", has 2 flat notes: Bb and following the arrow counter-clockwise to Eb.
Our Bb scale looks like this: **Bb C D Eb F G A Bb**.

Proceeding a 4th counter-clockwise to Eb we now need 3 flat notes to complete our scale.
Following the arrow we get Bb, Eb and Ab.
The Eb Major Scale: **Eb F G Ab Bb C D Eb.**

Things to Note About Flat keys:

- *The Major scales always contain 8 notes in alphabetical order.*
- *We always start on Bb when adding flat notes and then add additional ones in 4ths, or counter-clockwise following the arrow.*
- *The finished product ALWAYS falls into our Major Scale Formula: Whole, Whole, Half, Whole, Whole, Whole, Half.*

You'll find that over time the Circle of Keys will just happen for you naturally. I don't feel the need to make my students strictly memorize the circle because over time, it just well… happens naturally.

FAQ: GUITARISTS ON SCALES

Why do we need to practice scales as Guitarists?

If we as guitarists understand scales, we can easily learn the theory behind chords and other scales used to write songs, solos and improvise fluently in any style of music.

It also makes figuring out songs and solos from your favorite artists so much easier. Understanding the Major Scale and Key Signatures also enables you to read music in other keys besides C.

When we practice scales we are building a framework, or sort of mental highway that leads to all of the "good notes", other scales, arpeggios and chord forms.

It also makes improvising a breeze. Taking the guesswork out of jamming with your band, a backing track or other musicians is liberating. You can't do any of that well without some scale knowledge.

Why is Scale Technique Important?

Technique is a tool, and a very important one. Understand that how "good" a Guitarist may be to anyone is completely subjective. Technique however, is not.

Technique can be measured. It is almost quantifiable. It also makes every aspect of your guitar playing easier when practiced regularly.

Think of it as the most important tool in your Guitarist Toolbox. Sure you could hammer a nail with a rock, but having a good hammer is going to make every job easier.. forever.

How fast you play is optional. Whether you're into Blues or Progressive Metal, it just doesn't matter. Practicing scales will help you regardless of your chosen genre or how fast you want to get.

I learned all the Modes in Tuesdays lesson, why do I want to practice these scales too?

We're going to change it up today by using some different pattern types to confuse the right hand picking. Don't get me wrong, 3 Note-Per-String scales are the cornerstone of many modern Guitarists playbook, but by adding in odd-numbered notes per string we will develop a stronger right hand and also cover some of those weird little pockets of "good notes" across the neck for improvising and solos.

Think of it as the muscle confusion tactics taught by fitness professionals. Just when you're blazing through one scale pattern with ease, we're going to confuse those muscles by introducing a new, completely different picking pattern.

SCALE THEORY

As a 25+ year veteran Guitar Instructor, I've always tried to make theory as painless as possible for everyone. Sure, you could just learn the patterns, but a little knowledge will go a long way to making you a better musician as well as just a better Guitarist.

Major Scales and Modes: The Pentatonic Major, minor and Blues Scale.

You probably already know some these patterns. Typically they are among the first scales Guitarists learn… but did you know the theory behind them?

MINOR SCALE

If we take a regular Major Scale and start on the **6th degree** we get the Natural minor Scale (a.k.a. Relative minor).

C
D
E
F
G
A <<<——Start minor here!
B
C

A minor Scale: A B C D E F G A

Simple right? thats it! You just made a minor scale.

Take that newly create Natural minor scale and drop a few notes so that your left with:

A C D E G

After dropping the 2nd and 6th degrees of the A minor scale, we're left with a 5 note scale - **A Pentatonic minor**.

In relation to the Key of A Major you might also think of it as:
1, b3, 4, 5, b7

Remember in the C scale we went to the 6th degree to create our minor? Let's go back to the C and use these same notes but starting on C:

C D E G A

Now we have the **C Major Pentatonic Scale**! Boom, crazy simple right?
Don't over think it.. that's really all there is to it.

You might also think of this in relation to C Major as:
1 ,2, 3, 5, 6

Back to A Pentatonic minor for a second:

A C D E G

Now let's ADD a note. The #4 (or b5) - D#/Eb

A C D (D#/Eb) E G

This new 6 note scale is the **Blues Scale**.

Tip: All 3 of these scales are interchangeable within the key of C/A minor. Sure some will sound better than others depending on the chord progression, but they all WORK.

HARMONIC MINOR

This is a fun one! If you're into Classical Music, Spanish Guitar or the Neo-Classical Metal Guitarists of the late 70's thru 80's, you'll love Harmonic minor.

Back to our A minor scale for a second:

A B C D E F G A

Let's raise the 7th degree 1 half step.

G to G#

A B C D E F G# A

Now we have the **A Harmonic minor Scale**!

MELODIC MINOR

*I think it's at least worth a mention that there are 2 different ways to do **Melodic minor**. In Classical theory the scale is different ascending then it is descending. Sounds confusing right? It can be a little strange for sure.*

Let's check it out:

A Melodic minor ascending is an A Natural minor scale with a **raised 6th and 7th degree**:

A B C D E F# G # A

Descending, everything is set back to the Natural minor like this:

Backwards - A G F E D C B A

I've seen heated arguments about the usage of this "old" style Melodic minor. I've actually seen people say it is a myth or doesn't exist. My personal thoughts are that if it ever existed even ONCE, it is not a myth!

This old form was used widely through the Baroque era and into the early 20th Century. Somewhere along the line this methodology was dropped in favor of the modern Melodic minor scale more widely used today.

***Note:** The great Spanish Classical Guitarist Andres Segovia taught minor scales the "old" way with different ascending and descending notes. You can find them in his timeless Scale Book. So, it is definitely not a myth!*

MODERN (JAZZ) MELODIC MINOR

In the Jazz heyday of the 1940's-1960's Melodic minor was (and still is) widely used in improvisations to get a more sophisticated sound. I could do a whole other book on just that topic and it would still only be the tip of the iceberg… so for simplicity sake, let's see what happened in the 1900's.

Take your original C Major Scale:

C D E F G A B C

Lower the 3rd degree 1 half step

E to Eb

C (Jazz) Melodic Minor:

C D Eb F G A B C

It really is that simple! Don't over-think it.

Melodic Minor Shapes:

Here are some alternate fingerings for Melodic *(Jazz)* minor that I like to practice. The great thing about these is that the number of notes per strings feels bit random. This is great for mixing up that right hand alternate picking.

When you get all 5 of these down, you're covering the whole neck in new Melodic minor shapes. Grab a backing track and try using them in your solos and improvisations.

Ex. 1. 3rd Position: C Melodic minor

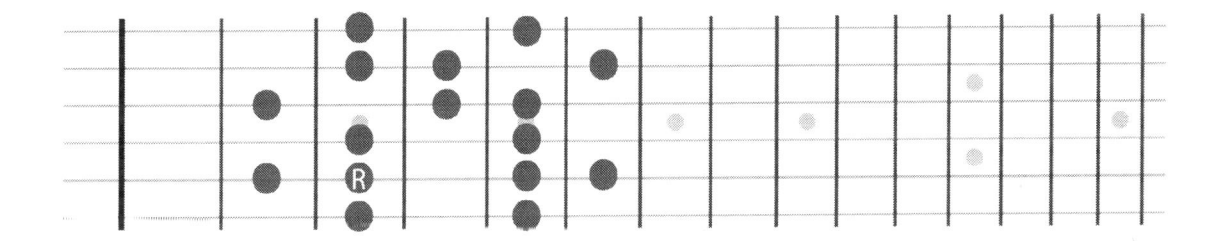

Ex. 2. 5th Position

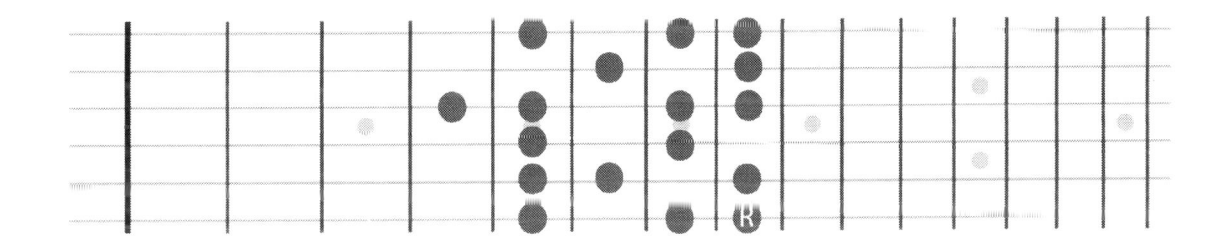

Ex. 3. 8th Position:

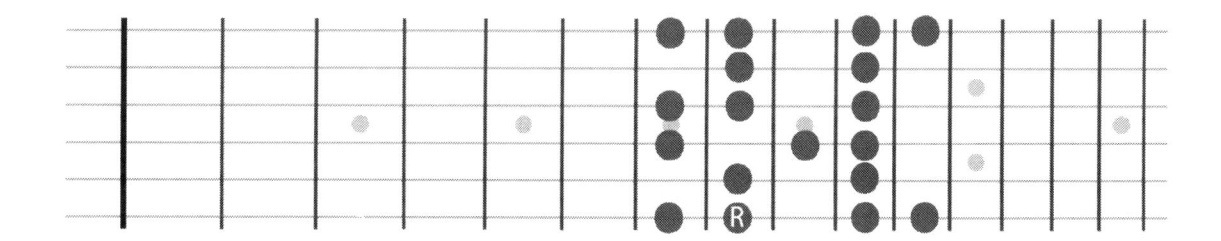

Ex. 4. 10th Position:

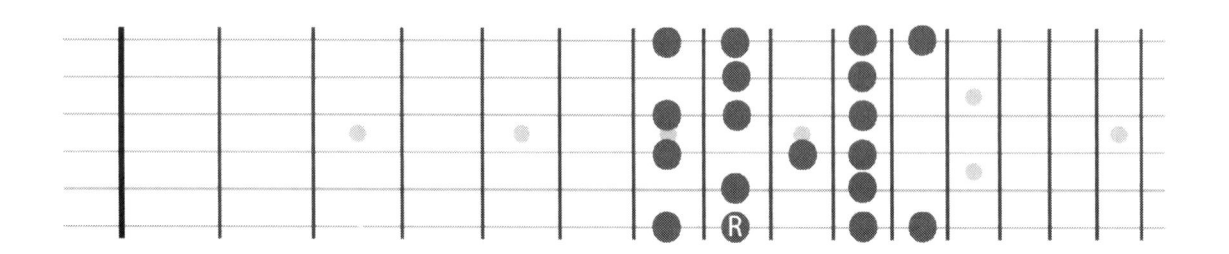

Ex. 5. 12th Position:

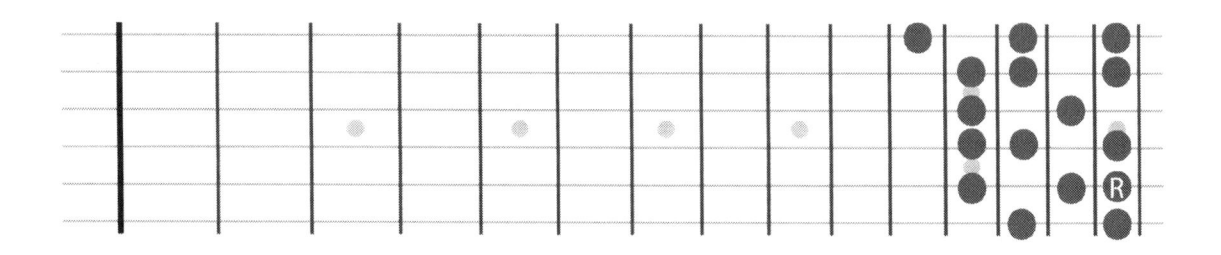

3 NOTE PER STRING MINOR SHAPES:

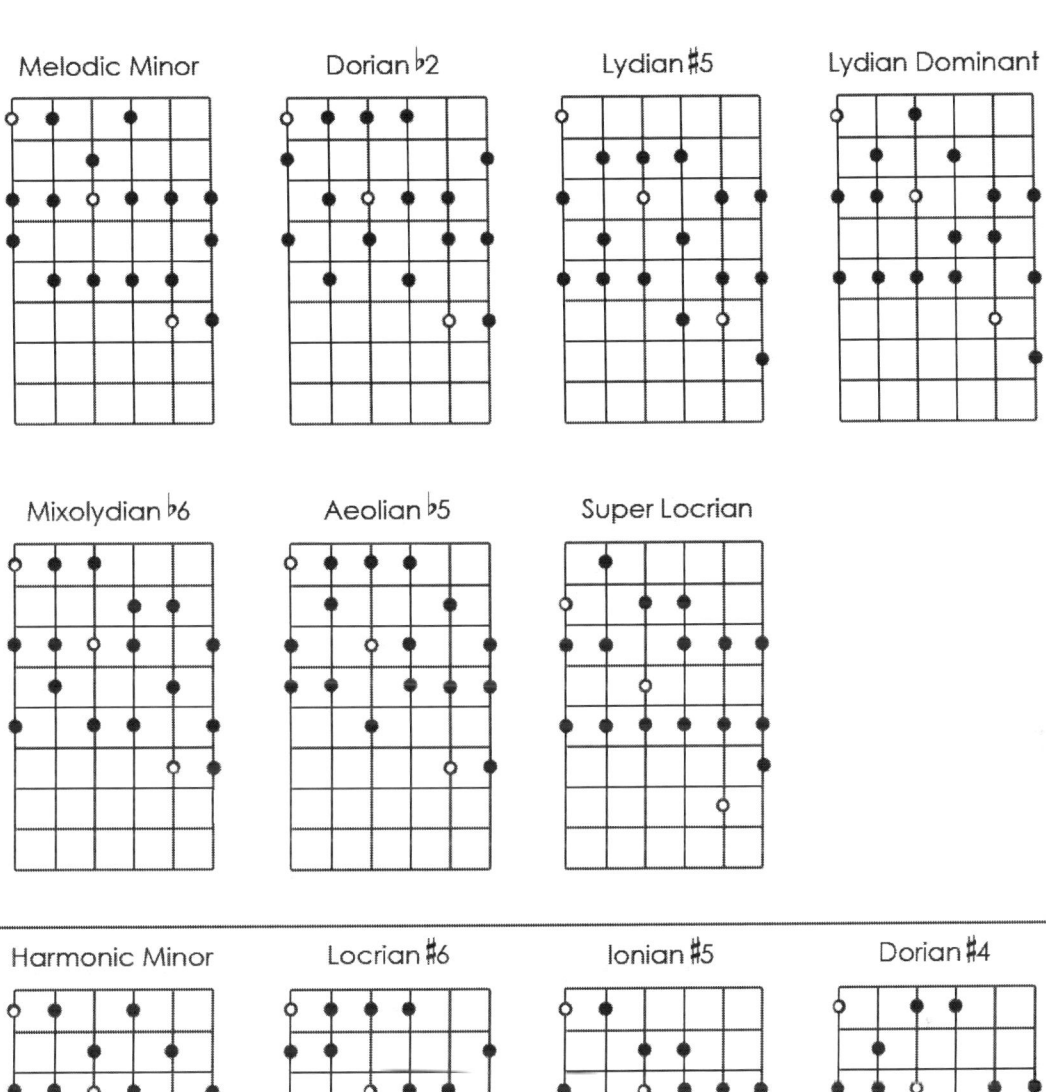

Melodic Minor | Dorian ♭2 | Lydian ♯5 | Lydian Dominant

Mixolydian ♭6 | Aeolian ♭5 | Super Locrian

Harmonic Minor | Locrian ♮6 | Ionian ♯5 | Dorian ♯4

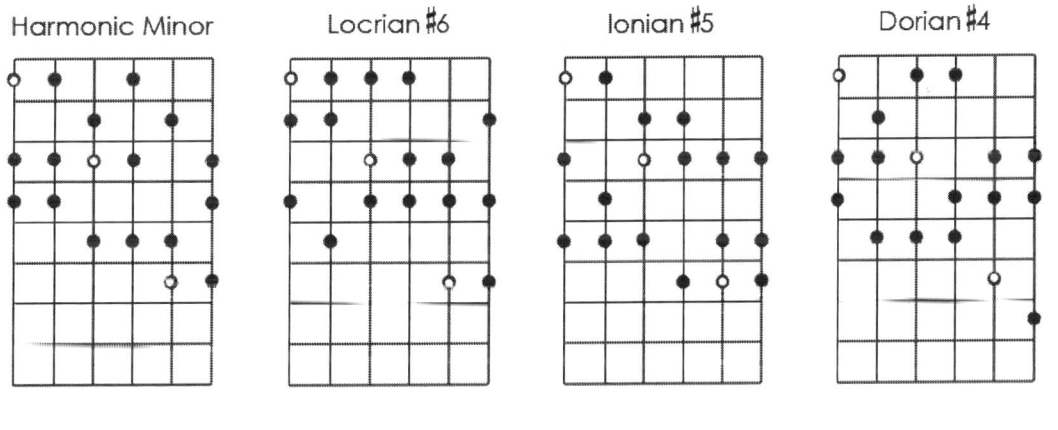

Phrygian Dominant | Lydian ♯2 | Diminished

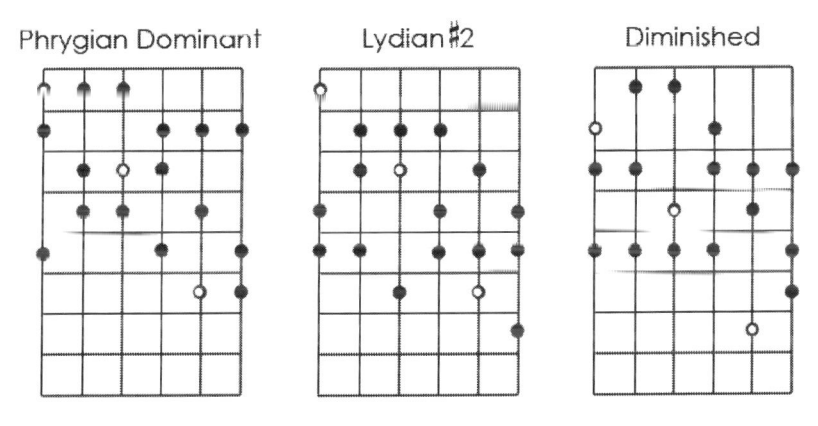

- *I know I've said it before, but ALWAYS use a Metronome.*
- *Go for 10 reps for each shape, but make them 10 PERFECT reps.*
- *For example if you mess up on the 10th one, do another or however many it takes to get 10 perfect ones.*
- *Practice slowly. Only practice as fast as you can play perfectly.*
- *Always alternate pick. After all, the whole purpose of this routine is to get the picking hand used to awkward string crossings and varying notes per string.*
- *Break it up. If the routine is too long and you're not quite ready, go ahead and split it over a few days.*

Examples *(Tab & Standard)* of the first shape in each series below. I've put them in a specific order for a reason. We want to do 1 shape, then move on to the 1st shape in the next series and so on.

The idea here is that right when your picking hand is getting used to the sequence, we introduce a new one with a different number of notes per string.

- A Pentatonic minor: 2 Notes per string.
- C Melodic minor: 2, 3 and 4 notes per string.
- C Pentatonic Major: 2 notes per string.
- A Harmonic minor: 3 notes per string.
- A Blues: 2 and 3 notes per string.

SCALE SEQUENCE EXAMPLE

Scale Examples

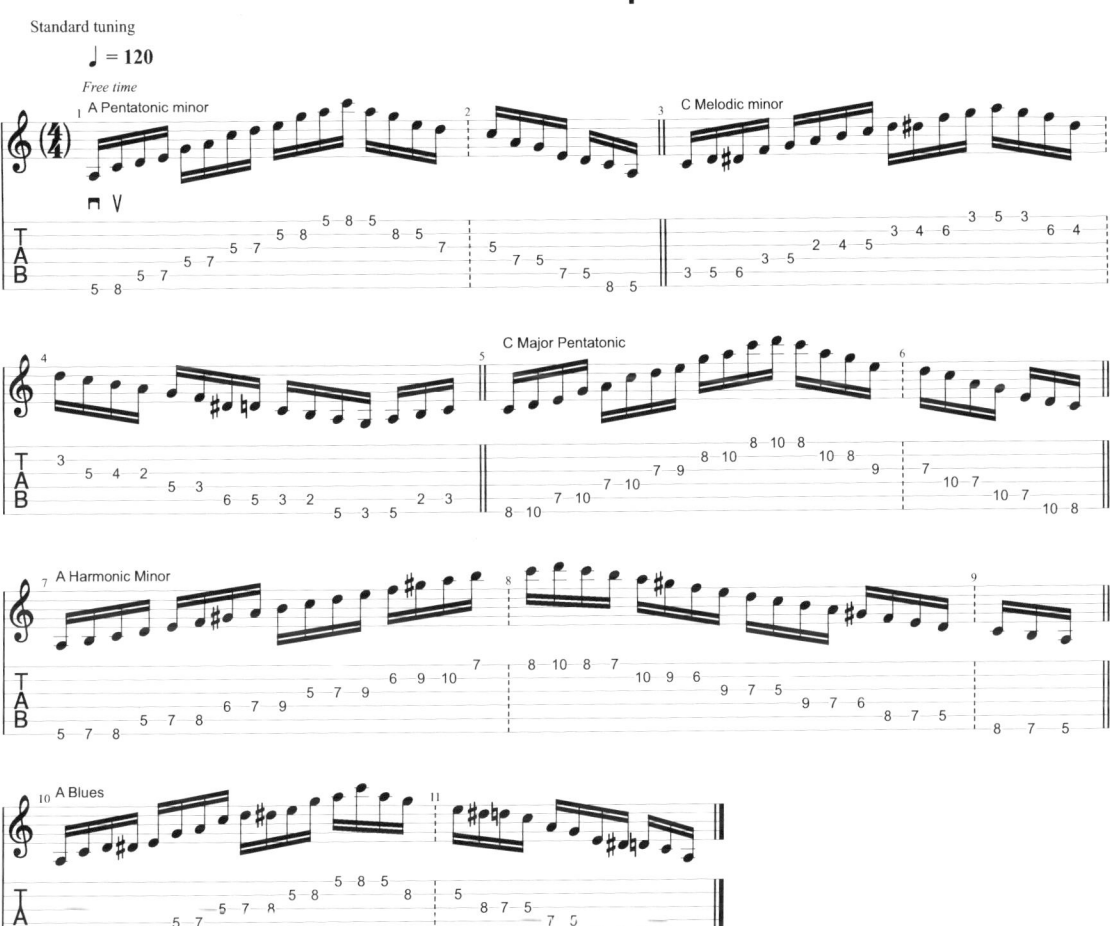

THURSDAY ROUTINE ROUNDUP

For the actual Guitar Practice Routine, we're simply going to do runs of each shape 10x each. I know what you're thinking, 10x each, that's it?

- *10x each, x5 Pentatonic minor. (circled root)*
- *10x each, x5 Pentatonic Major. (squared root)*
- *10x each, x5 Blues.*
- *10x each, x5 Melodic minor.*
- *10x each, x7 Harmonic minor modes.*

So that's 270 reps! It could take you anywhere from 30-90 minutes depending on the speed.

Scale Shapes:

FRIDAY - CHORDS

In days 3 & 4 we covered the theory of chords, arpeggios and basic diatonic harmony in the Major Scale.

Remember that from the Major Scale all things musical are derived. For the first example we're going to do some alternate picking through the chords in the Key of F Major:

F G A Bb C D E F

Chords in the Key of F:

I- F Major - F A C
ii - G minor - G Bb D
iii- A minor - A C E
IV - Bb Major - Bb D F
V - C Major - C E G
vi - D minor - D F A
vii - E diminished - E Bb D

Remember that the formulas for diatonic triads are as follows:

- Major - 1 3 5
- Minor - 1 b3 5
- Diminished - 1 b3 b5

Alternate Picking with Moveable Barre Chords.

Exercise #1
In the exercise below we're starting on the first note/chord of the F Major scale; F Major in the 1st position.

- Alternate pick through F Major.
- On your way back descending switch and alternate pick through Gm.
- Repeat and work it right into Am, Bb Major, C Major etc.

Ex. 1.

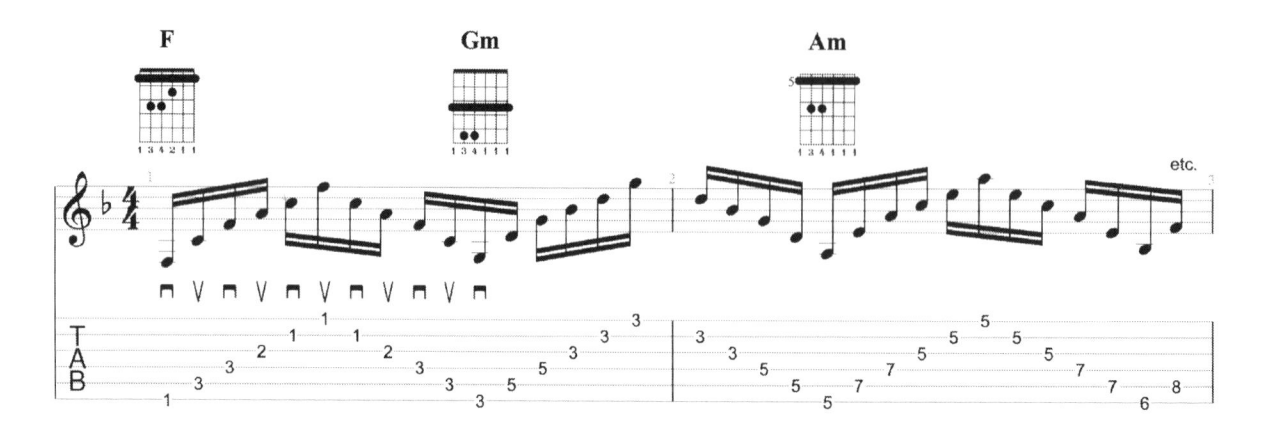

If you're a beginner and feel these barre chords are a bit too hard, thats ok. Try the same picking patterns using open chord forms. Gradually work in some 5 and 6 string barres until your left (fretting hand) feels strong enough to get through these routines.

7ᵀᴴ CHORDS

Ok let's Jazz it up a bit! Whether or not you're into Jazz or Jazz chord forms, practicing these shapes and routines will greatly improve your left hand strength and dexterity.

Rock Guitarists tend to ignore these shapes. If you're one of these people, don't! Learning difficult and unfamiliar chord shapes will propel your Rock Guitar Technique to new heights.

It will also enable you to start reading some more complicated chord charts for a gig or just for fun.

7th, 9th, 11th, 13th and altered chords are not something to be avoided either. Expanding your chord vocabulary will also enable you to get better gigs and stay a cut above other Guitarists who avoid it.

True Story:

About 12 years ago I was called for fairly high-profile, well-paying gig for a big production company in Orlando. At the first audition I got the gig because I knew how to play a Dominant 7b9. It was a simple D7b9 chord. No big deal.

The other Guitarist was a great player, but primarily a rock player. So was I, but the difference was, I could get through the chart and he couldn't … **and I got the gig**.

I made thousands of dollars on that gig which lasted over 10 years (the gig not the money). Now if you already know this stuff, you may be having a good laugh at that… if you don't know this stuff.. Let's get it covered right now.

DIATONIC 7TH CHORD STUDY

7th Chord Study

www.lifein12keys.com

Diatonic 7th Chords - Key of G Major

Let's switch it up to the key of G:

G A B C D E F# G

Diatonic 7th Chords in G Major

I - G Major 7 - G B D F
ii - A minor 7 - A C E G
iii - B minor 7 - B D F# A
IV - C Major 7 - C E G B
V - D Dominant 7 - D F# A C
vi - E minor 7 - E G B D
vii - F# minor 7b5 - F# A C E

Here we're going to do some quarter-note strumming. Keep it simple and try to get the shapes under your fingers comfortably before switching.

Play 2 beats *(or strums)* of G Maj7 before switching to Am7, Bm7 and so on through the entire scale. Use downstrokes to keep it simple until you feel comfortable with the switching.

Sounds cool right? 7th chords will really expand your chord vocabulary and give you some tasty substitutions for the common old Major and minor shapes you probably already know.

THE DIMINISHED "CONNECTOR"

Here is a great concept you can apply to 7th chords that will really make your chord progressions sound "jazzy". We're going to take a new chord, the Diminished 7th, and insert it on the off-notes between each chord.

That will look like this:

In Key of G:

G Major 7
————->>> OUT - G# dim7
Am7
————->>> OUT - A#dim7
Bm7
CMaj7
————->>> OUT - C#dim7
D7
————->>> OUT - D#dim7
Em7
————->>> OUT - Fdim7
F#m7b5

Here's what that looks like on paper:

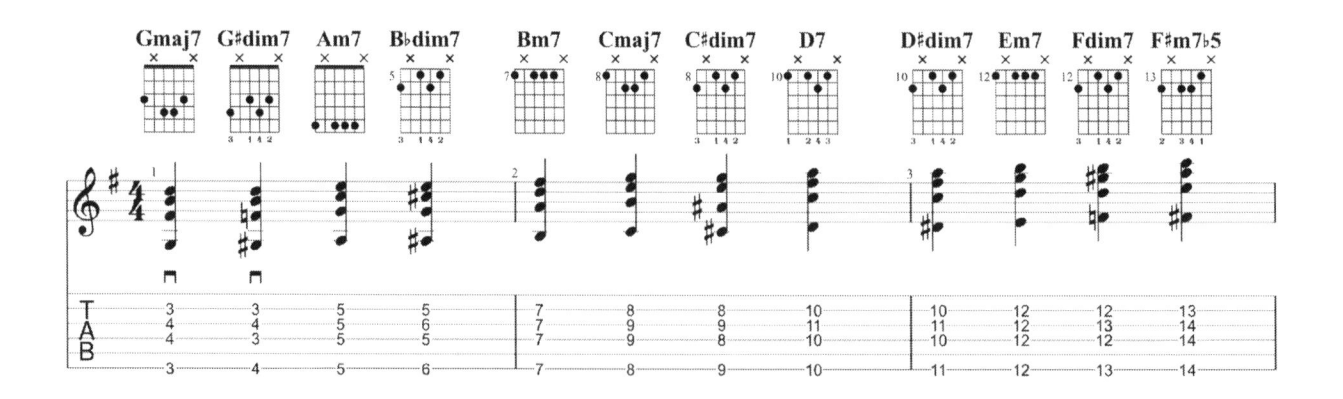

Other Chord Forms and Extensions:

You may be wondering, "ok, but what about 9th's, 11th's, 13th's etc"?

If you can count to 13, know your Key signatures *(which notes are # or b in any Key)*, you can create ANY chord if you know some simple formulas.

Take that G Major Scale we just played through above and number it up to 13:

1. G
2. A
3. B
4. C
5. D
6. E
7. F
8. ~~G~~
9. A
10. ~~B~~
11. C
12. D
13. E

We don't say things like 8ths or 10th's in Music theory, so let's cross those out.

You remember that a 1 + 3 + 5 always = a Major chord/arpeggio?
Now add a 7th and 9th to it like this:

G B D F# A - Now we've created a G Major 9

How about taking D7 and adding some extensions:
D F# A C = D7

D F# A C E = D9
D F# A C E G = D11
D F# A C E G B = D13

How about the mysterious and scary **Altered Chords**? Guitarists shouldn't be afraid of these either. Anytime we raise or lower the 5th or 9th of a Dominant 7th chord we are playing an altered chord form. **For example:**

D7b9
1 3 5 b7 (b9) <<—Formula
Notes: D F# A C Eb

How about something really scary?
D13b5#9
1 3 (b5) b7 (#9) 11 13 <<—Formula
Notes: D F# (Ab) C (E#/F) G B

The fact is, with some basic chord formulas memorized, you can make any chord, any time you want.

CHORD FORMULA MASTER CHART

Chord Formulas

Major Family

Major	1, 3, 5
Major Sus	1, 4, 5
Major 6	1, 3, 5, 6
Major 7th	1, 3, 5, 7
Major 9th	1, 3, 5, 7, 9
Add 9	1, 3, 5, 9
Major 6/9th	1, 3, 5, 6, 9
Major 7/6th	1, 3, 5, 6, 7
Major 13th	1, 3, 5, 7, 9, 13
Augmented	1, 3, #5

Minor Family

Minor	1, b3, 5
Minor 6th	1, b3, 5, 6
Minor 7th	1, b3, 5, b7
Minor 9th	1, b3, 5, b7, 9
Minor 11th	1, b3, 5, b7, 9, 11
Minor 7/11th	1, b3, 5, b7, 11
Minor Add 9	1, b3, 5, 9
Minor 6/9	1, b3, 5, 6, 9
Minor/Major 7th	1, b3, 5, 7
Minor/Major 9th	1, b3, 5, 7, 9
Diminished	1, b3, b5
Minor 7b5	1, b3, b5, b7
Diminished 7th	1, b3, b5, bb7 (or 6th)

Dominant 7th Family

Dominant 7th	1, 3, 5, b7
Dominant 9th	1, 3, 5, b7, 9
Dominant 11th	1, 3, 5, b7, 9, 11
Dominant 13th	1, 3, 5, b7, 9, 11, 13
Dominant 7/6th	1, 3, 5, 6, b7
Dominant 7 Suspended	1, 4, 5, b7
Dominant 7th Altered	1, 3, b7 with any combination of b5, #5, b9, #9, b11, #11, b13, #13

Some Thoughts On Chord Formulas

1) Think of anything containing a Major 3rd as Major, lowered 3rd as Minor and Major + lowered 7th as Dominant.

2) Augmented chords do not necessarily fit into any one category. We think of them as a Major type chord because of the Major 3rd.

3) Diminished type chords relate closest to minor types because of the lowered 3rd.

4) Memorizing every possible Dominant or Altered Dominant formula can be redundant. Knowing your Intervals on the fretboard and being able to visualize where to place a nearby altered tone in your Dom7th fingering is a much more useful way to increase your chord vocabulary.

5) Some Dominant 7th formulas are impossible to play on the guitar. For example the Dom13 contains 7 notes. Since most guitarists only have 6 strings it is acceptable to omit an ambiguous tone such as the 5th from your chosen voicing.

SATURDAY - CLASSICAL GUITAR 101

A Note From the Author:

When writing this book, I struggled with the idea of adding a Classical Guitar section. Classical Guitar is such a specific Guitar niche that I was worried about possibly alienating all of the Rock, Metal, Jazz and Blues players of whom I was sure would enjoy days 1 thru 5.

It occurred to me one day while practicing myself, how **important** Classical Guitar music is to my own playing. Furthermore, I feel I would be doing you, *the reader*, a disservice by not including it.

As I'm writing this chapter, I'm getting ready to do 6 gigs in a row this week. This month has been one of the busiest of the year *(October)*. While I always do my picking routines and chord/arpeggio studies throughout the week, often times when I have a busy schedule, I tend to neglect the fun stuff, which for me is Classical Guitar music.

I noticed something really important though:

When I'm not playing Classical Guitar, *everything else suffers*. I do mean *everything*. My left hand is certainly weaker and a bit of balance is lost between the two hands. Even my picking suffers.

The past 3 days I started working though some simple Classical exercises which I've outlined in this chapter. In just 3 days, here's what happened:

- *My left hand feels strong and more limber, particularly slurs. (Hammers & Pulls)*

- *My right hand, especially downstrokes, feel stronger and cleaner.*

- *Improvisation is better because I was reading actual music and not just tab. I'm better able to pick out the "good" notes in a scale or key all over the neck as a result.*

- *Chord grabs and switching is just easier and cleaner. Classical music is demanding on the left hand. When switching back to Rock, Pop, Metal, Jazz etc, everything just feels easier.*

- *It got me out of a rut. All Guitarists get into a rut from time to time. Working on something completely out of your comfort zone is a sure fire way to break out and progress faster.*

One common misconception is that finger-picking or Classical Guitar hurts or somehow doesn't benefit those Guitarists who are primarily pick-style players. This is inaccurate.

Finger-picking does much to benefit regular picking technique. Think about it… All Classical music utilizes the thumb for bass notes. The movement of the thumb moves in a sort of down and up pattern much in the same way you use a pick.

The index finger of the right hand is constantly pulling back like an upstroke. Also beneficial to picking technique. Transitioning back and forth between finger style techniques and pick-style will do nothing but improve the right hand for both styles.

CLASSICAL GUITAR SLURS: HAMMER & PULLS

Classical Guitar slurs are some of the best exercises you can do for your left hand. They build strength, speed and dexterity with only a small time investment per week.

Much in the same way we did 4-note-per-string exercises in Day 1, we're going to pair off every set of fingers on the left hand. The difference is, we're only going to pick one note followed by a slur or series of slurs.

SLURS

Ex. 1. Hammers

Ex. 2. Pulls

Ex. 3. Triplet Slurs

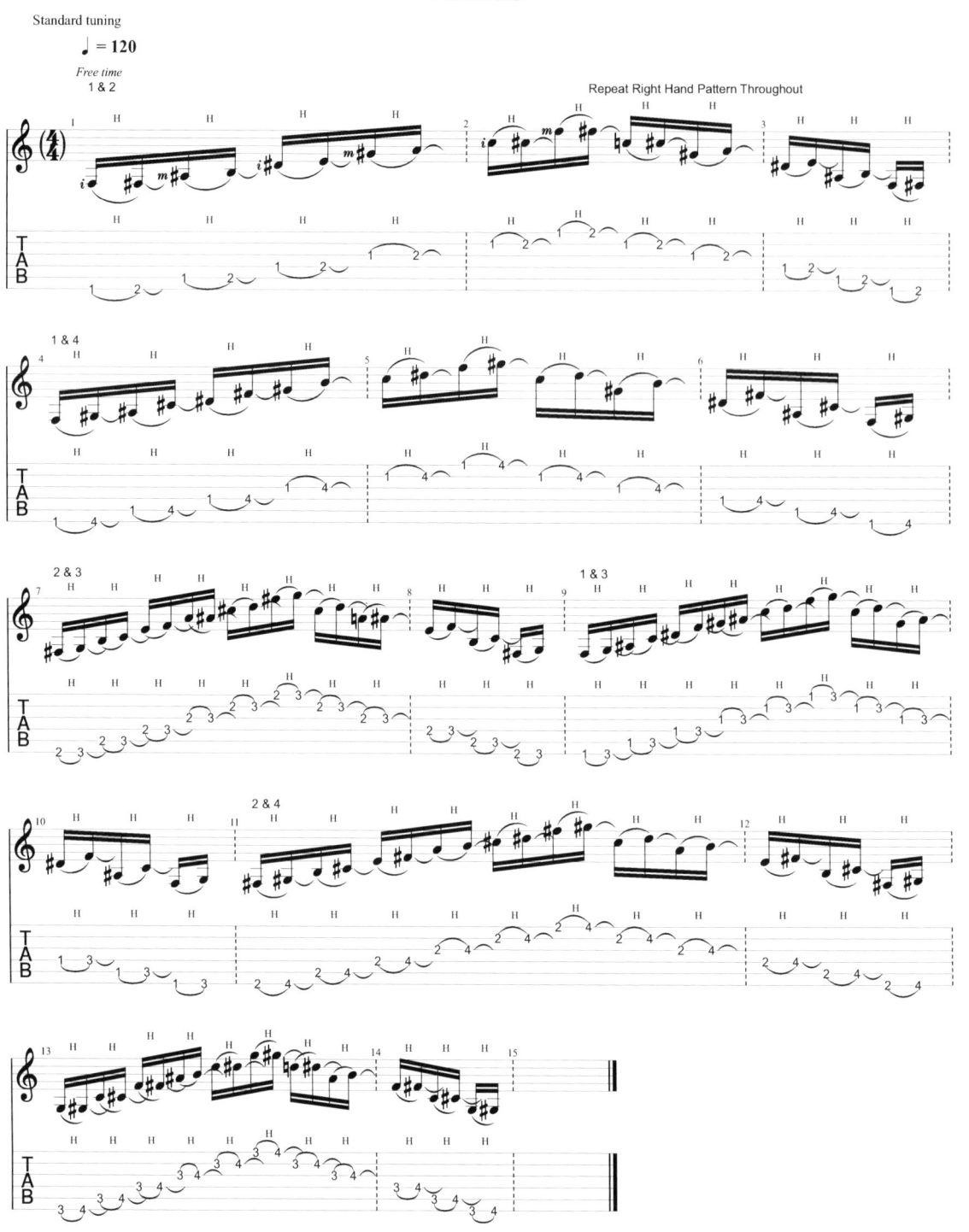

Classical Slurs
Hammers

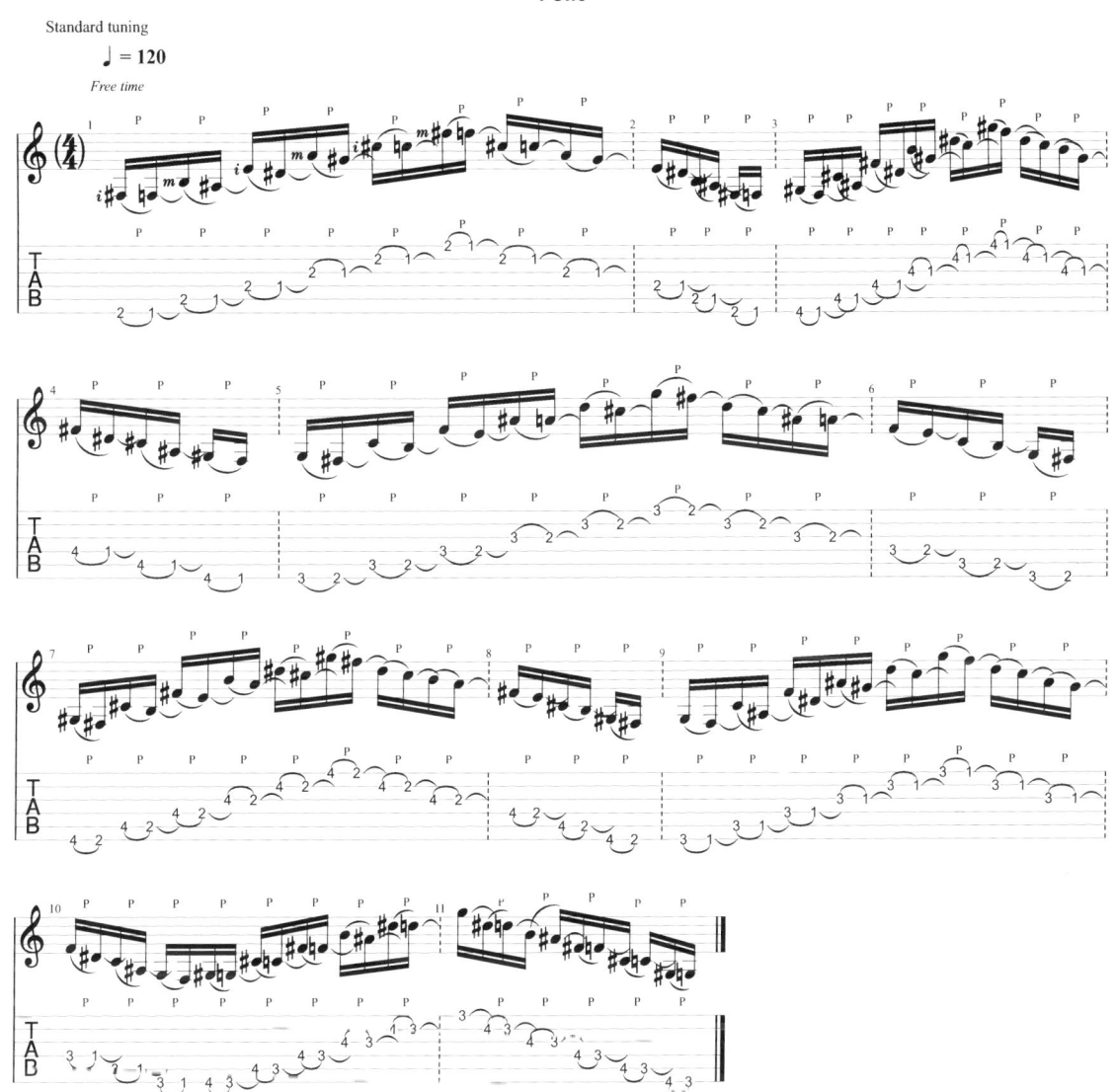

Classical Slurs #2
Pulls

Classical Slurs #3
Triplets

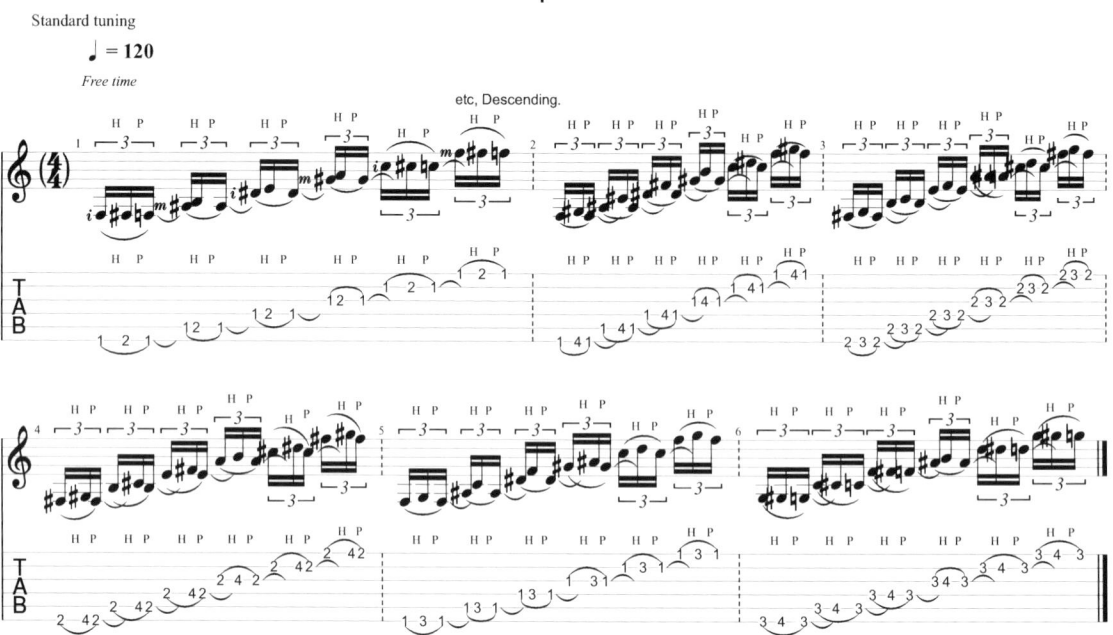

THE SPIDER SEQUENCE

This one is tough! Before you start, please be careful with this one and do not overdo it. If you feel any pain or discomfort in your left hand, take a break.

Here we're going to once again pair off fingers of the left hand. To set up, plant all 4 fingers in the 5th position on the G string. So, 1st finger 5th fret, 2nd finger 6th fret etc.

Next we're going to alternate pairs and move to the adjacent strings and then skip strings. For this one you'll have to finger-pick to pluck the notes.

Remember to keep the fingers not being used, planted firmly on the G String.

Spider Sequence:

Spider Sequence

SUNDAY - 120 ARPEGGIO STUDIES

Mauro Giuliani (1781-1829) was an Italian Guitarist and Composer who gave us some of the most beautiful and challenging pieces in the Classical Guitar Repertoire. While the majority of his compositions fall into the "Classical" music period from 1730 to 1820, his music was arguably more influenced by the Baroque period and much less from the "Romantic" period which followed.

We as guitarists owe essentially every useful right-hand finger-picking pattern to Guiliani and his 120 Right Hand Studies. Whether you're an aspiring classical player, or a rock or blues player looking to improve your fingerstyle playing, I think you'll find these studies an invaluable resource.

All 120 studies contain some form of a I-V progression in C Major. That is C Major and G (Dominant)7 in the open position. **See Figure 1.**

Practice the CMaj and G7 transitions to familiarize yourself with the left hand movements throughout these studies. Once you are comfortable with the chord changes, the right hand (*p, i, m, a*) parts will come naturally over time. While many of the studies are single note arpeggiated variations, there are many with multiple plucked notes as in Study #1 below.

Fig. 1

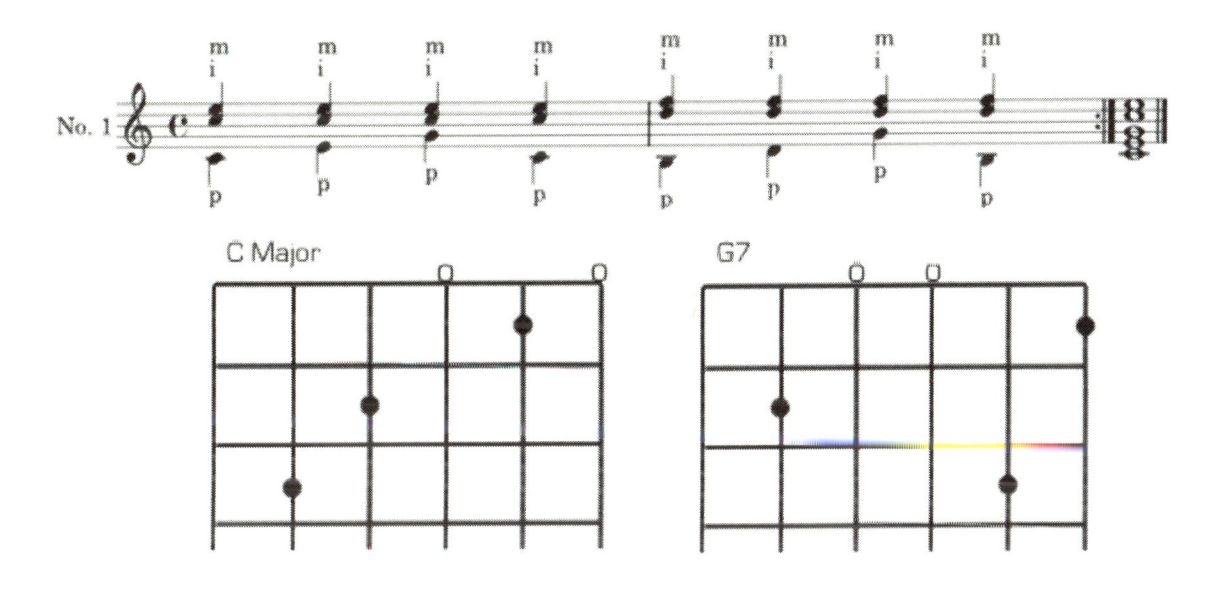

Practice Suggestions:

I like to practice these in groups of about 20-30 per day as a right-hand warm-up. This takes me about 30-45 minutes at a pretty good clip. At first you may want to start with only 2-5 per day and as the progression becomes more comfortable and the muscle memory kicks in, you might find yourself blazing through these pretty fast.

- Pay attention to the rest strokes on some studies.

- Do not play the right hand parts faster than you can switch to the next chord form with your left hand.

- Spend more time on the studies you have some difficulty with and less time on the ones which already feel natural to the right hand.

- **Take breaks often!** If you feel pain in your right hand wrist or tendons stop for a while and come back to it once the fatigue wears off.

I can't even begin to describe how much these often simple studies have helped my playing. 15-20 minutes on a few studies before starting your favorite Classical piece and you're all warmed up. There's a reason why these have been taught to countless guitarists for over 200 years! Enjoy.

Authors Note: *I've included all of the 120 Arpeggio Studies as a Separate .PDF download. It's almost another book by itself! Below are the first 8. If for any reason you didn't get your copy, let me know and I'll send it over.*
Email: craig@lifein12keys.com

120 Right Hand Studies

M. Giuliani

CLASSICAL GUITAR SCALES

Even though we've covered scales exhaustively in previous chapters, I think Classical Style scales warrant a separate section.

The primary difference a Rock, Blues or Jazz player may notice when playing Classical Style scales is the way the left hand shifts are presented. It just feels different and maybe even a little weird if you've only played conventional/modern style scales on guitar.

Andres Segovia, perhaps the most influential and well known Guitarist of the 20th century, wrote an entire book of his own scales in every key. I'm sure in the 1930's Guitar Scale books were scarce.

I think the whole point is to acquaint the left hand with a different type of shift. We can illustrate this using only 4 different shapes. After you're comfortable with these, I'll leave it to you to move them into other keys.

Ex. 1. C Major - 1 Shift, 2 Positions.

In ex. 1. we're going to play a C Major Scale starting in the 2nd position. Once you've played the B note (4th fret, G string), we then shift to the 5th position and complete the second octave of the scale.

Ex. 2. D minor

In the D minor scale example, we're only shifting once.

Ex. 3. G Major
Ex. 4. A minor

In examples 3 & 4 we're covering 3 octaves with several left hand shifts. Pay close attention to the left hand fingerings and work through these very slowly.

Classical Scales

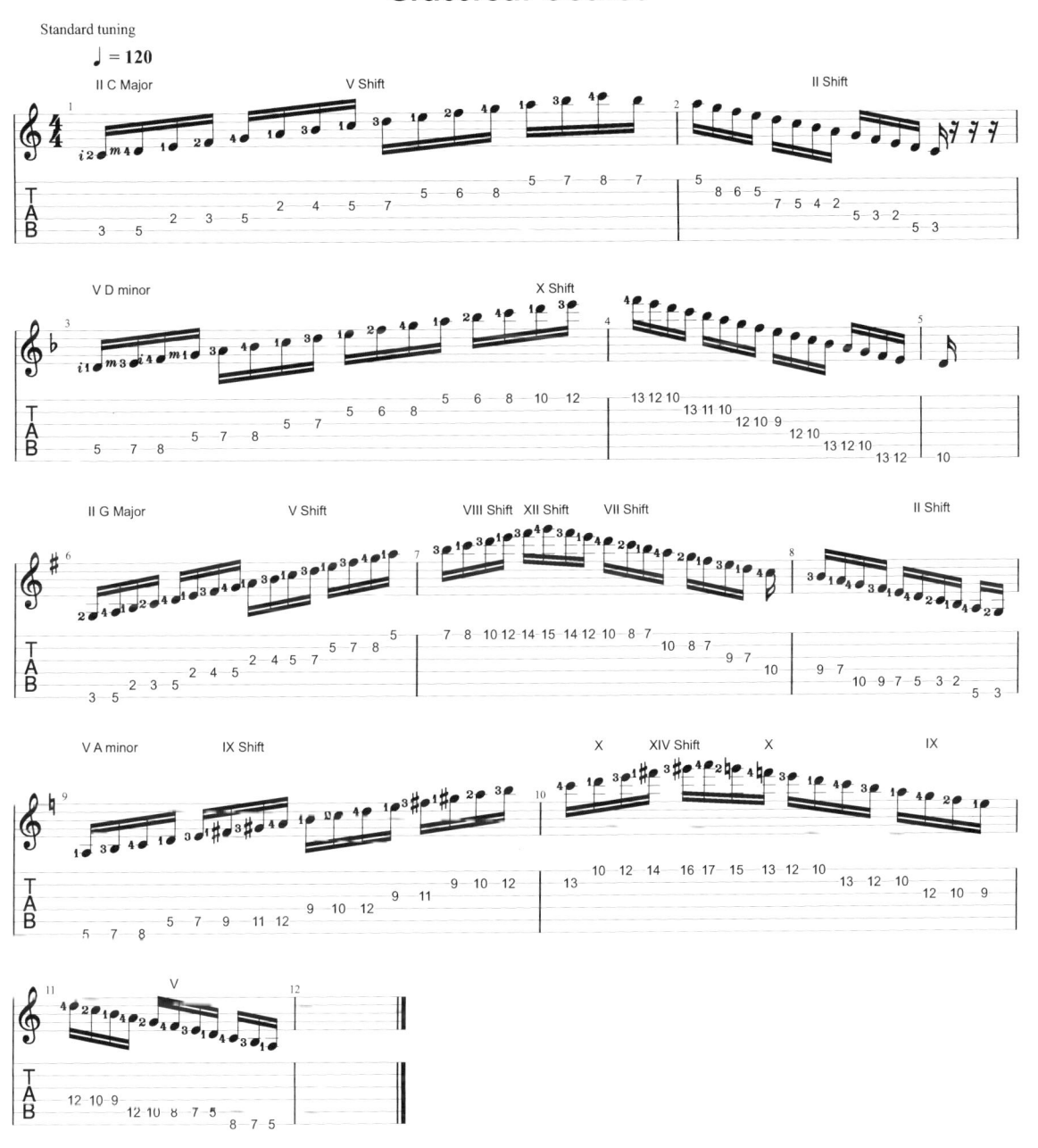

Remember to alternate right hand fingers:

1. i,m,i,m
2. m,i,m,i
3. i,a,i,a
4. a,i,a.i
5. p,p,p,p

Tip: *If you're completely new to finger-style or Classical Guitar, stick with alternating (i,m) for a while until you feel comfortable. After that, go ahead and work in the other right-hand combinations.*

CLASSICAL SCALE STUDIES

BOURREE
J.S. Bach

BACH'S BOUREE IN E MINOR

Johann Sebastian Bach 1685 – 1750) was a German composer and musician of the Baroque music period. He is known for instrumental compositions such as the Brandenburg Concertos and the Goldberg Variations as well as for vocal music such as the St Matthew Passion and the Mass in B minor.

Since the 19th-century, he has been generally regarded as one of the greatest composers of all time.

After you're comfortable with some Classical style scales and arpeggios, why not give the Bouree in E minor from Lute Suite #1 a try. While not a beginner piece, it is often the gateway to Classical Guitar repertoire for Guitarists of different genres.

Tips:

- Work through the piece one measure at a time.
- After memorizing 1 measure, move to the second and then play both.
- After memorizing 2 measures, move to the third and play all 3.
- Repeat this process until the entire piece is memorized.

Repeats and Sections:

- Play to the end of bar #8, move back to the repeat sign at bar #2.
- During this second cycle skip bar #8 and start section 2 at bar #9.
- Play to the end of bar #25.
- Start repeat at bar #10 and continue to the end of the piece, while also skipping bar #25.

BEGINNER CHORD FORMS

Open Position Chords

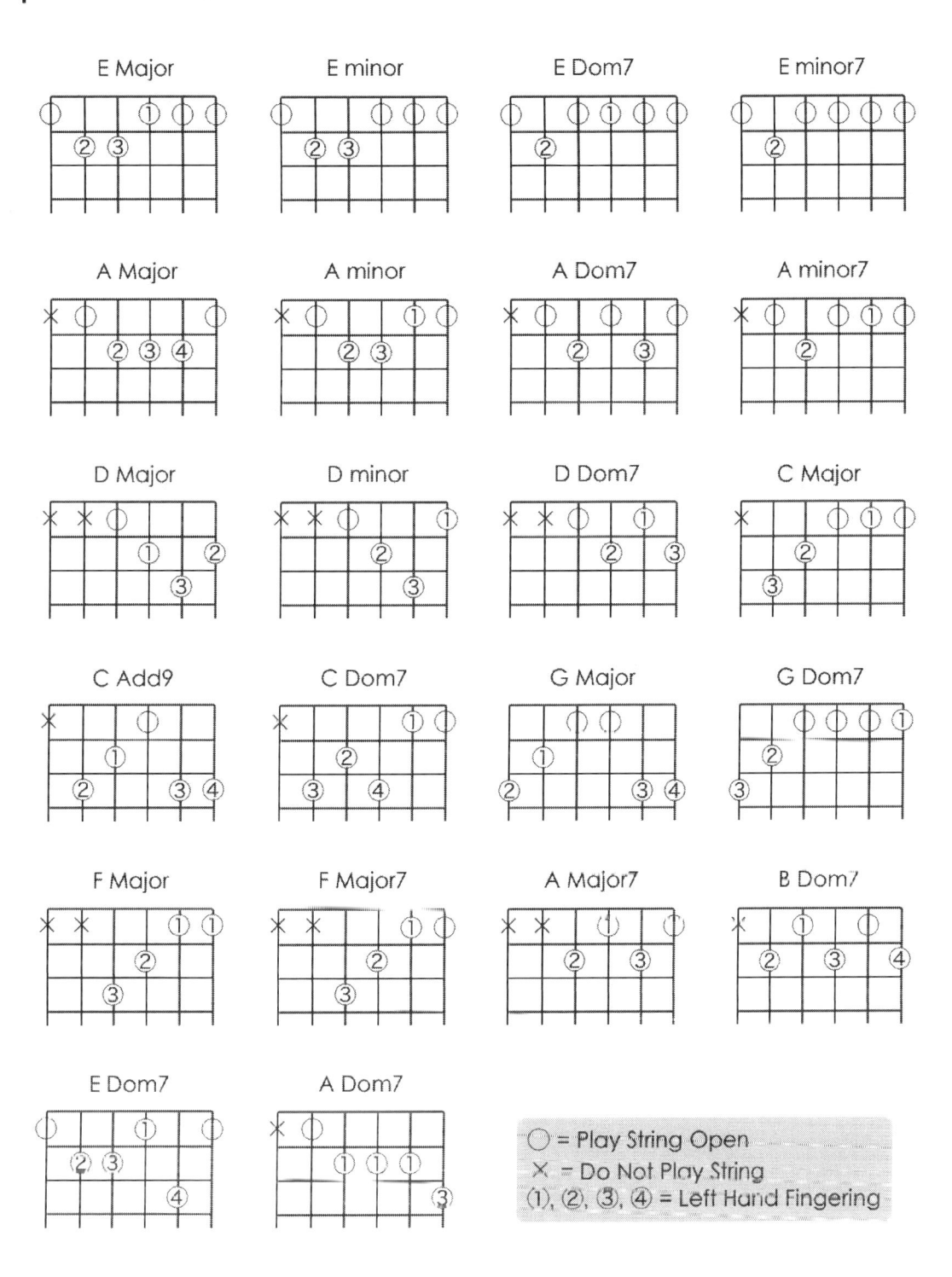

E Major   E minor   E Dom7   E minor7

A Major   A minor   A Dom7   A minor7

D Major   D minor   D Dom7   C Major

C Add9   C Dom7   G Major   G Dom7

F Major   F Major7   A Major7   B Dom7

E Dom7   A Dom7

○ = Play String Open
✕ = Do Not Play String
①, ②, ③, ④ = Left Hand Fingering

BARRE CHORD FORMS

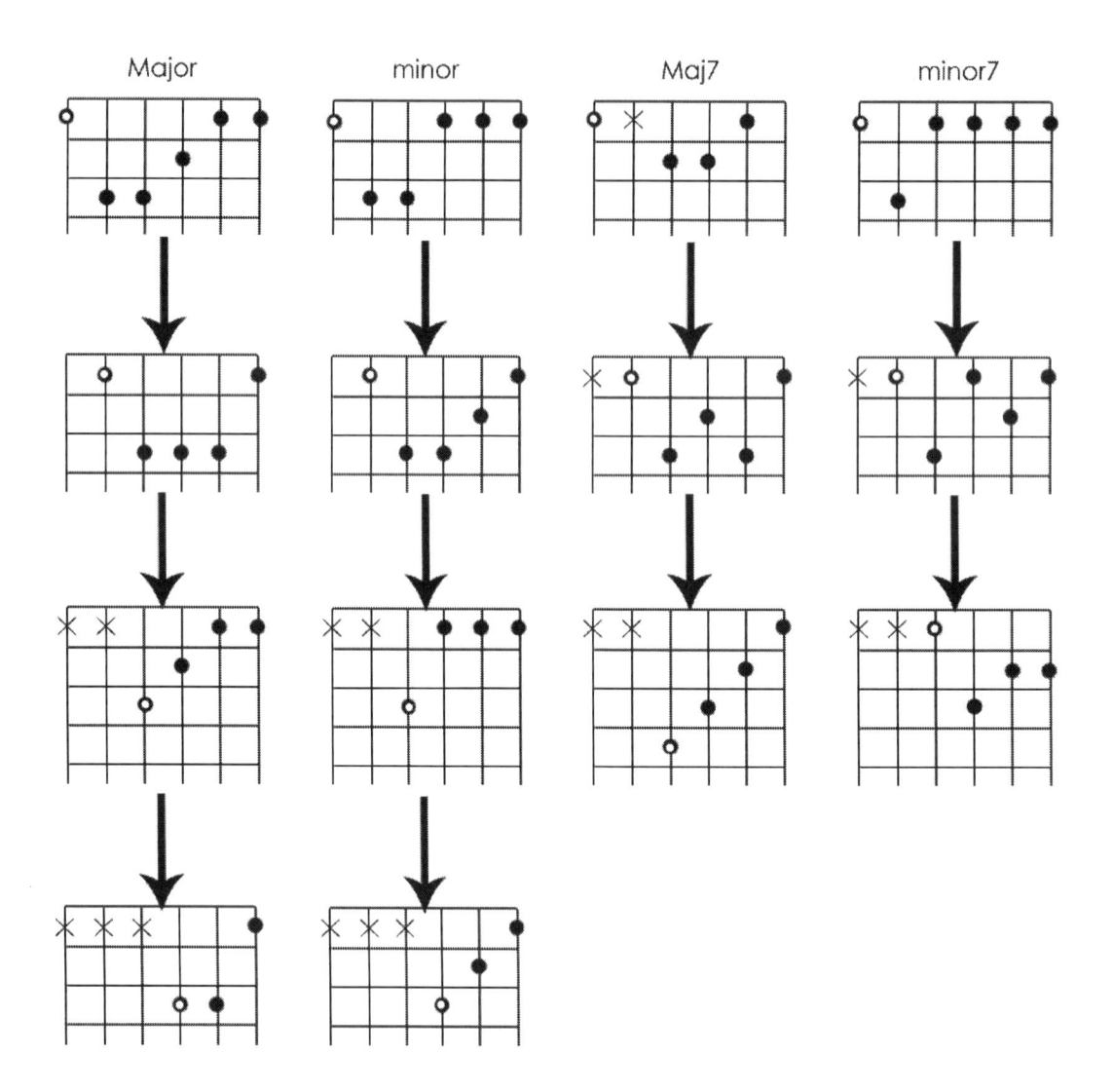

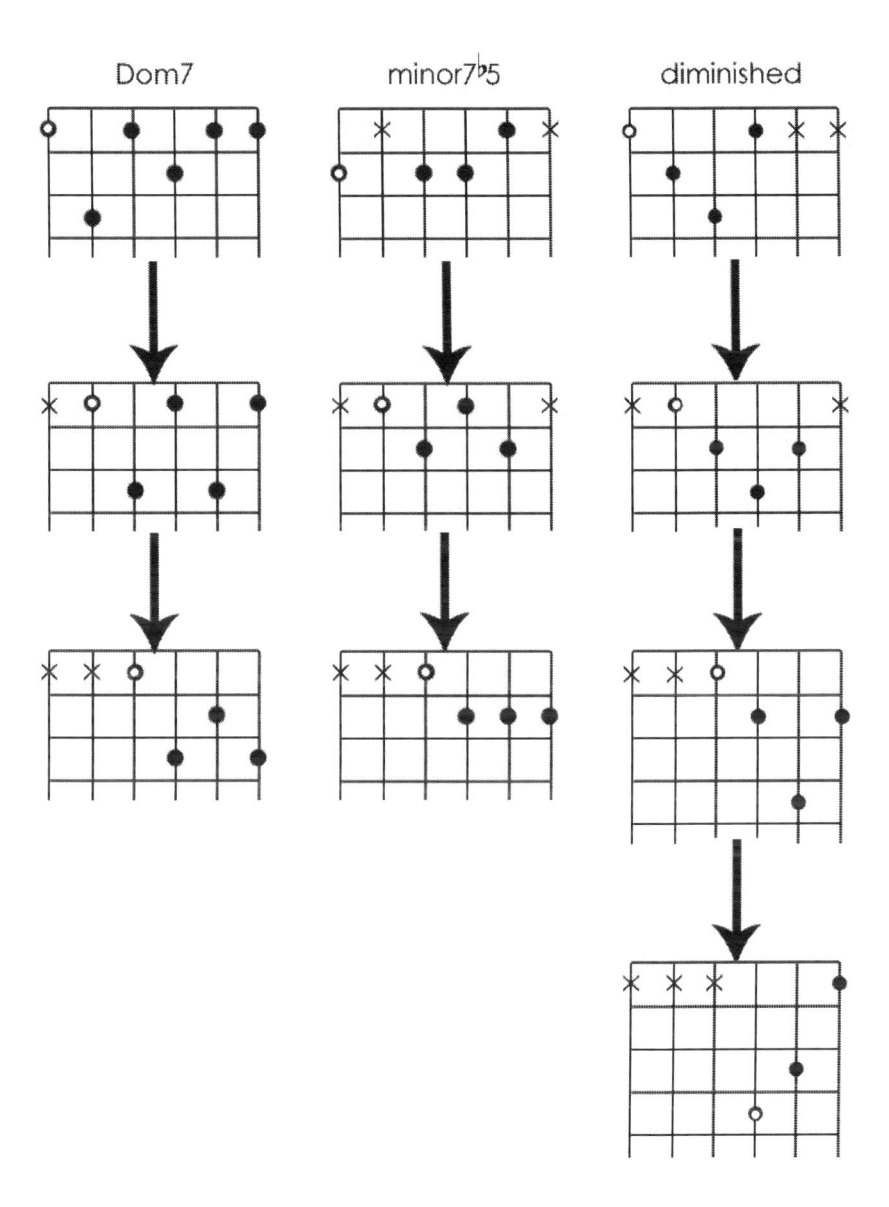

PENTATONIC MAJOR, MINOR & BLUES SHAPES

Circle + Dot = Minor Root
Square + Dot = Major Root
Hollow Circle = "Blues Note"

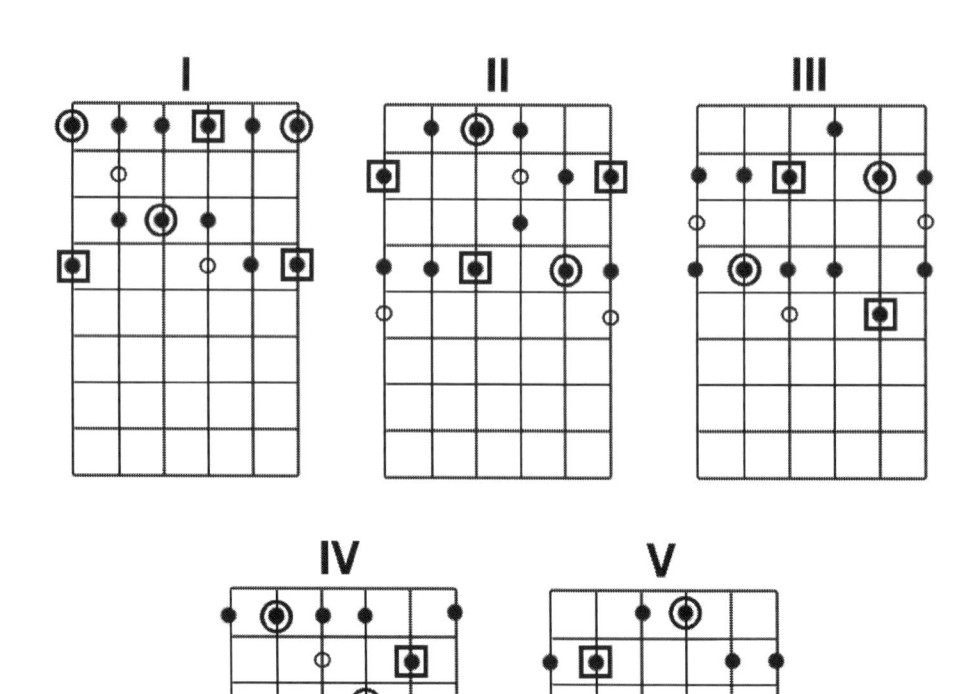

AFTERWORD

GUITAR PRO FILES:

I've included links to the Guitar Pro 7.5 Files for all of the music examples in the book.

http://lifein12keys.com/bookaudio

All files include full audio, TAB and Standard Notation. You can also speed-up, slow-down and even edit these files on your Mac, Windows or iOS Devices.

If you don't have Guitar Pro, I highly recommend it for every Guitarist.

Use My Link Below for a Free Trial:
http://lifein12keys.com/Guitarpro

ABOUT THE AUTHOR

Craig Smith has been a Professional Guitarist and Teacher for nearly 28 years. Originally from Canton Ohio, Craig grew up during the heyday of 80's Guitar.

After playing in Rock, Metal and Pop bands for over 10 years, he moved to Florida in 1999 and quickly became a first-call session and live Guitarist in Orlando, Florida.

After teaching for many years and thousands of gigs, Craig is still out performing 4-6 days per week around Central Florida. He lives in Sanford, Florida with his wife of 21 years Celeste and their four Chihuahuas': Yngwie, Abigail, Rosita and Princess Leia.

When he's not playing guitar live, he's blogging and helping other Guitarists online.

Website: www.Lifein12Keys.com
Contact Email: craig@Lifein12Keys.com

Manufactured by Amazon.ca
Bolton, ON